# ASCENDANT THOUGHT
## A New Seth Book

# ASCENDANT THOUGHT
## A New Seth Book

### By
### John and Dotti McAuliffe

This book is manufactured in the United States of
America. Design and cover art by Bradley W.
Dehner. Distribution by The Talman Company.

      The Tallman Company
      150 Fifth Avenue
      New York, NY 10011

ISBN # 0-912949-09-0
Library of Congress Catalog Card Number 87-050114

A
Uni ★ Sun
BOOK

# TABLE OF CONTENTS

This edition brings out several different approaches toward governing the output of thought energy in ways that could prove to be beneficial to individuals and the planet as a whole. By use of some of these methods, one can establish patterns of thought that will channel energy of a "right kind," serving to fulfill one's true desires.

Authors' Preface . . . . . . . . . . . . . . . . . . . . . . . . . . . . . . . . . . . v

Introduction by Seth . . . . . . . . . . . . . . . . . . . . . . . . . . . . . . . vii

Chapter 1    The Essence of Thought . . . . . . . . . . . . . . . 1

Chapter 2    Use of Thought . . . . . . . . . . . . . . . . . . . . . . 17

Chapter 3    Variables of Thought . . . . . . . . . . . . . . . . . 33

Chapter 4    Dissecting Thought . . . . . . . . . . . . . . . . . . . 51

Chapter 5    Why Thought Is Important . . . . . . . . . . . . 69

Chapter 6    Grouping of Thought . . . . . . . . . . . . . . . . . 79

Chapter 7    Interrelationships of Thought . . . . . . . . . . 95

Chapter 8    Neutralizing Thought . . . . . . . . . . . . . . . . 113

Chapter 9    Redirecting Thought . . . . . . . . . . . . . . . . . 125

Chapter 10    Control of Thought . . . . . . . . . . . . . . . . . . 139

Chapter 11    Composite . . . . . . . . . . . . . . . . . . . . . . . . . 161

Chapter 12    The End Result . . . . . . . . . . . . . . . . . . . . . 169

# DEDICATION

*This book is dedicated to the spirit, Kryon, who is teaching us that love and truth make all things possible and whose influence brought this book into being.*

# AUTHORS' PREFACE

John and Dotti came together at a time when their individual growth seemed at a standstill. John was a salesman and Dotti was a hair stylist when they met. John was channeling various energies for himself and was the inventor of a few energetic spiritual devices. Upon meeting in San Rafael, California, Dotti wondered why John would keep this information to himself and she proceeded to bring in other individuals for the growth of all.

Their lives took on a completely different path within a year, which brought a close personal relationship. It wasn't long before their jobs were removed and they dedicated themselves to the full time pursuit of spiritual growth. There were three children involved, who were quite surprised to suddenly see the influence of various spiritual entities in their lives.

It was not long before the voice of a spirit named Kryon was heard in their home, sometimes a little louder than would befit the comfort of all. After some time, Kryon sounded as if he might be borrowing some teachings from another entity. This entity would be known by the name of Seth. After testing the energy at a channeling session, but not identifying himself directly, Seth then emerged and stated that he wished to write another book.

Up until this point, Kryon had introduced Seth prior to his speaking directly through the channel. At this time, Seth started to come through directly and has been active in writing this book and teaching at various channeling sessions and personal readings.

As this book was written, the authors actually lived it in such a way that they would begin to understand its concepts. The information in this book has contributed much to bringing them closer and giving them freedom from the emotional stress that formerly would have been driving forces in their lives.

This book is written to help those who are struggling, as the authors have struggled, attempting to overcome patterns of thinking that would slow their spiritual growth.

# INTRODUCTION BY SETH

This new book, written through John and Dotti, begins to dig into some of the broader aspects covered in previous editions. Many of the new concepts on thought presented here were alluded to in other writings but the actual clarification of some ideas was left open until now.

Thought then was delved into in an exploratory manner, but the minute delineation was left for this volume. This would be an age in time that would benefit greatly from the exposure to these concepts.

Using a different channel (John) to voice ideas involves adjustments that would cause some anxiety for beings. Dotti, taking the spoken words in and instantly putting them into finished form, found herself adjusting rather rapidly to a new system of recording. It would not be so easy for beings to adapt, hour by hour, listening to an entity who would be known for writing many books and trying to work in concert with his delivery. Formerly in time, that would have been the job of the late Jane Roberts. A diligent recording of the energy and cadence of someone not of this world is not so easy.

As I have written in other volumes, I continue to make use of certain words in a way that would *jar* the reader's attention so that the concepts presented would not *lull* them to sleep. One of the difficulties that I would have going through a new channel and a new publisher would be to convey the message from out of time using words in a way that there would not be rules to apply!

Some of these words are "now, then, would, might" and others which would seem to be redundant. There would be a very important reason for using these words. Books have energy and channeled books, specifically, have a certain cadence using specific words that would keep the flow of energy or thought in sequence. If one were to use rules that were designed to deal with language in time, the same rules would not apply to the direct transmission from an entity not in time. It just will not work. The use of the word "now," for instance, is to keep the reader in the now moment. The various words I would mention have a specific category to remove the influence of time and would be important to the transmission of a message. Without these words, the message would lose its meaning.

In this volume, we would cut down on the use of comments in order to make use of another method of expression, that is, more directness.

There would be some unpublished material or transmissions of mine that would find their way to the printed word at this time.

Working, then, with this channel would prove interesting for me for it would involve the sharing in time or a joint space, if you would, with other entities who would have various thrusts of disciplines leading beings to the same spiritual growth. Working in concert with these entities of course would add to, not take from. Several would use very strong magnetic energy to promote growth and healing. Others would use color and musical sound to advance meditation and other spiritual abilities. Flowing in concert with such energies adds to the greater enlightenment of beings.

Now, a reason to bring forth the information in this book at this time would be in concert with what is taking place on your dynamic and rapidly changing planet. In the probable future, as seen through your eyes in time, many perhaps frightening events would be predicted. As seen through the eyes of others, cataclysmic change would be predicted, coming to devastate your planet. Many would respond with thoughts of fear, not knowing any better avenue of escape. The idea of cataclysm is only one of thought and in a way that I will explain in this book, the control of thought in effect enables one and all to control cataclysm. What I would say here is the word "cataclysm" has but relative meaning.

In this book, I would use the being known as Dotti in conversation and John and Dotti's three children, Mia, sixteen, Johnny, fifteen and Danielle, ten, to assist the reader in understanding the various concepts presented.

# CHAPTER 1

## THE ESSENCE OF THOUGHT

Now, thoughts are things. Thoughts are all that we are. If one has a thought, then dependent upon the emotional charge that is manifested along with the thought is the degree or the time in which it takes the thought to come into fruition. Now, there are other countervailing forces which also come into play. If one thought, "I want a sum of money," and nothing was in the way, then nothing could stop the sum of money from being presented to the one who had the thought. There are many stories to the effect that someone thought something and, surprisingly, it manifested. They might say that this was but an idle thought. But in the absence of any counterbalancing force, it would come into being. So if thoughts are things in essence, then one goes about constantly creating. This idea has been "known" for some time, but what is not known is the actual mechanics, if you will, of the process. So, if one thought of an object, then it would be automatically created unless there was another thought which would keep it in abeyance.

Now, many thoughts are not kept track of by the conscious mind. Let us say that ten years ago, one had the thought, "I wish I had a blue car." Let us say that the thought was swift and passed with little memory of it. Ten years later, one suddenly is looking at cars and would just have to have a blue one. Now, where did this idea come from? This is a more simple idea of what sometimes is a bit more complicated succession of events which leads to a particular result.

Now, where time comes into focus with thought is the amount of emotional charge that is placed with it. If the same thought, let us again say, of the blue car, is repeated over and over, impressing more and more emotional charge, then the length of time until it manifests becomes shorter and shorter. Unfortunately for beings, this seldom works directly because other thoughts get in the way, sidetracking the issue. Let us say, now, that one has a thought and something would interfere, such as a loud noise, a telephone call or any other interruption. These interruptions have the effect of postponing in time the acutal manifesting of the thought. Another force that comes into play would be the level of vibration of the being manifesting the thought. What would be the difference between a master and one of his students? It is only a matter of time, you see.

Now, let us say that one somehow is able to raise his vibrations to a degree that the time factor is shortened, so instead of taking ten years between thought and result, it would be, say, three days. What have we done here? Do you know?

*"You can suspect that there is a way of putting in feeling, along with a thought and in some way that I don't understand consciously, the thought is then manifested."** 

That was a brilliant answer. In a way that I will explain, eventually, this is the exact process. It is no mystery, of course, to concentrate, visualize and impress the thought in some greater part of you and then by letting go of it, it then becomes fact. Now, the part of you that the thought "lands in" is the part that will determine the amount of time and where this will happen.

The place where thought lands governs the amount of its travel. The amount of its travel governs the amount of time until the thought has what I call enough intersections to bring the event about. A thought which would land in an area of lower vibration would necessarily have to travel a greater distance than one which would be placed into higher vibration, the lower vibrational thoughts then being much slower in speed than the higher. This would encompass a great deal more travel in space and time

*Dotti's responses to Seth (channeled by John) are shown in italics.*

and would involve many more intersections or events. A slower, lower thought would encounter much more resistance and would be impeded in its travel. If this could be viewed in terms of light, it would not have much light shown upon it. Now, I didn't say speed of light. When I speak in terms of light, I wish to disconnect an absolute, relative speed. I speak in a way that the light is bent in many directions, slowing its progress. One of the influences that would slow down its progress is time. If you would measure the speed of thought, one would encounter thought traveling from a relatively low rate to that of infinite speed. At the lower vibration, the thought would be bouncing from obstacle to obstacle, creating much resistance and picking up much space and time. At a higher vibration, if one could reach this level, then the thought could be at infinite speed and, therefore, be instantaneous.

Most beings would put limits of time on their thought. By putting time limits on thought, beings would seek to speed it up when, in essence, they slow it down. If one would have a thought and then let it go, it would manifest at infinite speed. The difficult thing, of course, is learning to let it travel at infinite speed. Do you know know to do this?

*"The difficult thing is to let go."*

But I have already tricked you, haven't I?

*"How did you trick me?"*

By use of the word "do" instead of "be."

*"Oh, you really have to stay on your toes around here!"*

(Seth Laughs.)

If you "do" anything, then it dramatically slows it down. When you are being, then you have let go and the thought is then at infinite speed. Do you know what I mean?

*"I know what you mean with time. If you're 'doing,' you're in time. If you're 'being,' you're in timelessness."*

Yes, that is quite correct. But, how do you get into timelessness with your thoughts?

*"If I could answer your question, I would have few problems."*

(Seth conducts an experiment.)

Now, we have taken a little walk, haven't we? We have gone to a very high point. You wrote a thought on a piece of paper and we have placed it in a very decorative box and closed the lid. You then drop the box, with the written thought inside, over the edge where it could never be retrieved. Now, what you have done is let go of the thought into being at infinite speed. The thought now *is* (into being). Do you understand?

*"Yes."*

Now, for reasons I will explain later, the thought is now golden, isn't it? The golden keys to success. Gold seems to have a particular ring to it. So, maybe one would be at the top of the mountain or high place at the time of a golden sunset, symbolically. This then sets the thought into motion.

This thought is now a thing and it sets into motion a series of events leading to its most probable result. Now, the universe being infinitely intelligent, it will then intersect into the shortest probable result.

This thought then goes out and bumps into or intersects with other events or intersections, forming a path or string which then brings the result forth. If one were to attempt consciously to understand how this came about, it would defy your imagination. It would seem that "out of the blue", someone or something sent the completed thought to you in a disconnected or mysterious manner. In essence, the universe merely took the shortest probable path to manifestation.

Now, the thought was put forth and it just "happened" to bump into another being's thought, which was being manifested for the same purpose or another. This intersection then chained into another intersection or another thought on its way to manifestation. It would seem, in no time, that there would be a myriad of thought intersections going in every direction to completion.

An example comes to mind. When you had a need to sell a car, you were driving down the road one day and you missed or were late for an appointment and you suddenly decided to make the trip worthwhile and go elsewhere. You decided to stop at a store and "out of the blue," someone who worked there said to John, "Do you wish to sell your car?" In essence, the thought had been put out and let go of and the car was already sold, prior to your arriving at the store. Is this what happened?

*"Yes, it is."*

Well, I guess I've proven my point, haven't I?

Now, all of this was accomplished in a vacuum, wasn't it? How could anyone ever explain the series of events that intersected with this result? Well, what happens is like putting a thought into an all-knowing computer and having it spit out the result after much mixing and matching. That, in essence, is how the universe works.

Now, surrounding your planet, imagine successive layers of particles. Each particle is a colored thought particle with some sort of electrical charge. Each thought particle has a degree of intelligence. Some are more energetic than others. Each thought has a relative charge that corresponds to the relative vibration of the planet as a whole. In other words, each thought has an attraction of like kind on the planet. Each thought has a number of variables which are: Electrical charge, Magnetic attraction, color, speed and a relationship to other thought, as well as something called *stuff*. This is a relatively intricate network in that all is controlled by an intelligence. If a certain thought is put forth with the "right" variables, then it could attract another of the same variables at any distance or time. If variables were right, a thought from someone in the year 1565 A.D. could intersect with someone in the now moment. Does this sound fantastic?

*"I have heard of this, but do not understand why."*

Let us take a few examples. If you suddenly think of a friend, it is most probable that the friend is thinking of you, also. If your vibrations are high enough, then the thought could be quite strong and there would be communication. This could be with or without the aid of an artificial communication device. If the energy is charged enough, no device is needed. This, of course, is known as telepathy. So, in essence, there is a level of thought that is attracted infinitely. At this level, communication may actually be engaged. Let us say there is an emergency that would produce strong energy or thought. Someone thousands of miles away, if closely connected, may actually read the situation and take appropriate action.

Now, you and John have such a connection, do you not?

*"We do have this connection."*

There have been times whereby one senses the message of the other several miles away without the aid of anything but telepathy. This, in essence, is a bond at a very deep or high level of energy. At this level, thought, of course, is at a very rapid speed. At other times, events or weather are known in advance. Is this not so?

*"This is true."*

In the case of weather, it would seem to indicate that storms might be thought of as collections of thought. Have you ever thought of this?

*"No."*

Now, all information is available all of the time. It is only a question of attracting it or tuning it in. If enough emotion or false thought is "put aside," then its restrictive influence is out of the way, allowing in a greater amount of information. It is in the calm, still light that one can view from the observatory of the infinite.

(Seth conducts an experiment.)

Now, John, being a channel, has a tool at his disposal that one might not at first recognize. Do you have some idea of what I mean?

*"I have seen John forecast the weather accurately the last two nights."*

Unknown to John, this ability was suddenly opened to him. It is in the way of a strong feeling. Did you get a little suspicious when he carried the umbrella from the house to the car when it wasn't raining?

*"I figured it was going to rain."*

The worm hole that I slip through is the same as the one the "weather channel" slips through. So, this experiment worked. Do you think the local weather bureau would hire him?

*"Probably not. He does not have the accepted credentials for the job. No one would believe it. But I can certainly make use of this ability."*

Now, I have conducted an experiment. I have actually proven that advance probability is available somewhere. Much attraction of like kind of information is available. You would think that thought might be available in many forms. Now, what catalyzes thought? Are there particles of information? What would happen with music, for instance? Is it charged thought? Something obviously attracts it. This can then present a whole new concept of what thought is. Have you thought about this?

"*No.*"

Does a rock communicate with you?

"*Sometimes.*"

In what way? You had a favorite place where you and John used to go to meditate. Information from a variety of forms was presented, was it not?

"*Yes.*"

All right. It would seem that information is available in a form that is not understood. Now, thought is put out and has a particular number of characteristics. Available information also has characteristics similar to it. There just happens to be an intelligence that matches the thought with information. If one floats the thought out with sufficient charge, the intelligence is then matched to the thought particle.

(Seth gets up and pounds the wall hard, then softly.)

One you heard, one you didn't. What do you think the difference was between the two?

"*One had more energy than the other.*"

Was one more intelligent than the other?

"*No.*"

Was it thought that was put out or was it just energy? Obviously, it was just energy. But, the energy did have a degree of intelligence, didn't it? Your receptor would tell you that it meant a certain sound, of the fist hitting the wall. So, here we are now saying that energy has a form of intelligence, are we not? Now, does all energy recognize all other energy? Yes, it does. One being would recognize another of like kind, but would also recognize an animal. If the animal was unknown, it still would be recognized as an animal. In some way, one rock would recognize another rock.

*I start laughing, thinking of this.*

Obviously, the point is that everything is energy and all energy has an intelligence. Now, how would one form of energy attract another? Each energy particle puts out a projection, let us say *stuff* and is capable of receiving the same.

Now, this would seem to indicate that thoughts would be more complex particles than energy particles. Does this make sense to you?

"*Yes.*"

Thought would then have a rationality to it. That is, it may have several different attractions to it with the corresponding number of receptors. Let us say this thought is put out in a coded form that universal intelligence recognized and interprets so that attractive energy is then imbued to coalesce with the thought, bringing its attractiveness into manifestation. Each thought, then, would have a number of electrically charged parts in coded fashion sufficient to bring the thought to completion. Energy and thought then both could employ what in time could be called telepathy. Some part of all energy, then, is infinitely intelligent. Some part of all energy knows about all energy to the degree that it is charged. In this place, then, time and space are not required. The supercharged thoughts would then go to this place and in this place, time would not exist. Time is a factor, however, for the thought to escape from time and re-enter it. Sometimes the thought may have sufficient energy to leave time but not to re-enter it. Sometimes its velocity is such that it will leave time and will not re-enter time for some time. One could have a thought and it might come back two hundred years later. Thought might re-enter in the form of a dream or a vision or just plain thought. Now, think of all the thoughts that are available to think with.

Without a code to unravel this seeming complexity, the sorting of this mechanism would be impossible. Each code is a recognized potential to universal intelligence. It is like going to a warehouse with a requisition. The requisition is colored or encoded according to the potential placed in it. A "white" requisition would receive a "faster" response than a "brown" one. The coding process would automatically color it according to its potential. If the "white" were bright enough, then instantaneous response would be indicated.

Now, the level of the sender would determine the amount of force or velocity needed to whiten the thought. A true master would send out all white thoughts. Others would send out different shades, determined by the energy *released* with the thought.

Let us take two separate beings. Let us call them Joe 1 and Joe 2. Joe 1 has many problems. He has much anger and has a difficult time with everyone that he runs into. His life is a struggle and he has constant ailments. Joe 2 lives next door. Joe 2 is in perfect health and has a harmonious relationship with nearly everyone, including Joe 1 next door, but Joe 1 does not know it. This statement is particularly important to realize, for note the difference in viewing that the two contain. Their economic condition is relatively the same, but their harmony with their environment is diametrically opposed. Joe 2 thinks primarily in "whiter" thought while Joe 1 is a "brown" thinker. This does not mean, of course, that either one is incapable of other modes of thought. This would be indicative of their primary mode of behavior or essence of thought. Truly, though, lines of demarcation need not be drawn.

Do you think that Joe 1 and Joe 2 would have anything in common, such as friendship?

*"I don't think they would have very much contact with each other."*

Now, interestingly enough, Joe 2 could be a friend to Joe 1, but Joe 1 could not be a friend to Joe 2. This is coming from the relative viewpoint of each being. Another way of looking at it, Joe 2 would contain consciously all of the thought of Joe 1 and then some. Joe 1 would be consciously more limited.

So far, as you have adroitly indicated to me privately, we are only dealing with one thought at a time. Do you think there would be more than one conveyed at a given now moment?

*"Yes."*

Now, what happens is the higher the level of thought, the more singular in purpose or potential it is. In most cases, however, thought or thoughts are strung together. Take the thought which you mentioned, "I want a new car." You might attach a coincident thought to it that states, "I don't know if I can afford it," or "Make it a red one." Along with this thought, you might have added, "I want four doors." You might throw in a whole mixture of things that you want. The effect of this might tend to delay the implementation in time.

Now, let us say that you wished strongly to break a habit. First of all, to let go into singular thought, one need convince oneself that what one is thinking is truly what he wants. Let us take a habit and call it defiance. Let us say that this particular habit has been one that would rule someone for most of his incarnation. The habit is so entrenched that at times it is not even known to exist. Behavior is exuded that stems from a source that is unknown.

Out of the blue, one suddenly becomes reluctant to work on a project and begins to find excuses and all manner of delay to avoid the completion of the project. The slightest interruption would be an excuse to go with the interruption and have it follow into another until hours or even days would go by. Now, the interesting thing, also, to the defiant one, would be that everyone around him would join in the act. How could this be? Obviously, the thought is put out and others pick it up. They know on some level that the message has been put out and they don't even know why it is that they are free to cause all manner of disturbance and interruptions. Children may suddenly start squabbling and it is not clear from whence it started. Surprisingly, even your dog may get into the act. She may all of a sudden decide to extract her pound of flesh. The phone starts ringing and a long conversation is then in store. Those who might work with you would also get into the act. They might decide that the project was really not very important, after all. What has happened here? Without a spoken word, you have told everyone and everything to defy you. One thing leads to another. Anger and frustration result in further delay. All of a sudden, the project becomes onerous and something to be avoided at all costs.

When thought is put out, the one who places it seldom realizes from whence it came. If I said the word "defiant" to you, what would follow?

*"Trouble."*

And if I used the words "followed by," what would you say?

*"Nothing."*

There appears to be a little block in the way of defiance, doesn't there? Then, if I say "underneath this?"

*"Fear of being pushed around."*

By whom?

*"Them."*

Who is them?

*"Anyone who might expect me to do something."*

Something?

*"Type this book."*

Is this not the very thing you wished to do?

*"Yes, so long as it was my idea."*

So, anyone who would ever wish to share anything with you

would first have to know about defiance and understand some way to help you believe that the idea came from you. This is clearly circular thought, is it not?

*"Yes, I guess it is."*

What have we shown here? That thought is chained together in a way that if you had the keys to follow it, it might lead to a boomerang effect. Did you know this?

*"I know it now."*

What would you do if you again felt like delaying?

*"I would ask myself why I am being so defiant about doing the very thing I want to do."*

All thought may be chained together in this manner. So, when the thought is put out, "I want a new car," one might think in a more specific manner. The question then comes to mind, what is behind the thought?

Can you imagine the thought that is put out in this confusing manner? When someone asks you a question, what is behind the question and what is the motive? Are they asking you for the reason that they ask or are they asking for a reason only known to them? Then it becomes a matter of you deciding what it is that they ask. When John asks you, "Do you wish to go get some wood?" what is he really asking?

*"He's telling me that I have to go get some wood."*

That is strange. I thought he asked you.

*"It sounds like he's asking, but I think he's really telling me what to do today."*

So, how would John ask you if he could join you to get some wood?

*"I'm confused."*

Yes, you are confused because your thought intermingled with his in a way that substituted your thought chain with his question. If John then said, absentmindedly, "It is a nice day," your next thought would be, "He would do anything to force me to get that wood." So, this thought chain is so ingrained that any of one thousand words would get the same result.

Now, let's go back to the question of the new car. It now takes on new meaning, doesn't it? Seeing the chain as it is in place, what might you add to that thought? Of course, you must throw out a defiant thought. It is part of your makeup. Now, what would the universe bring into manifestation?

*"It wouldn't be a car."*

Maybe it would be a new, red "Defiant." Now, the universe does have a sense of humor about thought and it might be surprising to see what the new, red "Defiant," if there was such a brand, would look like. As you indicated, someone might leave a pair of red roller skates or a new, red tricycle on your front porch. Then you would wonder why they did that and the person who left it would wonder, also.

As I have already suggested, all energy is chained together, as I have attempted to describe, in a way that clearly provides the completion of a summons.

Now, let us say that enough beings started conveying the thought that it will rain. There are forces in place or collections of energy coinciding with time that would have it rain in certain months, probably, anyway. Coalescing with the implaced energy is the collective thought of many beings deciding that it "should rain" sometime. The requisition is then implaced and to the surprise of few, it rains. Another way might be to seed clouds already in place. Still another might be to use collective thought symbolically, in the form of a rain dance. This also would work if the directed singular uniform thought was placed strongly within the universal coding system. Some adepts could clearly manifest rain with but little effort. Now, if other thought were strongly placed with enough energy such as the type of storm, like thunder, lighting and high wind, then the energy of the storm will respond in kind. Now, this energy could be in the form of fear. Fear is powerful energy and could result in what you really don't want. But the thought has been put out so strongly that it is manifest. "I fear a flood" or "What if there is a flood?" A storm builds and then fear takes over. The storm builds. Fear builds. The storm adds energy. Fear adds more. This could go on and on until a balance is achieved and the storm, in effect, releases the stored up energy. Now, you could say that a real good storm would vent the energy of pent up fear and frustration. This is exciting and is clearly a transfer of thought energy from one form to another. This is a common occurrence and goes on with but little understanding of the process.

Along this same line, the fear thought, being quite powerful, could generate another kind of storm. Have you any idea of what this might be?

*"It could generate a storm inside a person in the form of anger and he would blow up, changing the energy or releasing it."*

Now, each thought creates. What would a defiant thought create?

*"I don't know."*

Would it not create defiant thought in other beings? If the thought then came to another being, "Aha, a defiant thought," what would the reaction be?

*"The other person would become defiant."*

What would be their choice?

*"They'd have no choice."*

So for every action (thought) there is a reaction, if the energy has intersected and coalesced. So, this force which is thought then interacts in a manner that would create another thought which would oppose or add to the energy of the first thought. What would follow? This would go on until the energy put forth would balance and be vented in some manner.

We have now learned that energy put forth in the form of thought is then balanced in some manner to afford completion. This goes along the line of the thought, "As I reap, so will I sow; as I give, I receive." Now, if you are defiant, you receive defiance. One could wander through life encountering nothing but defiance or anger from other beings and would be mystified or believe that other beings are this way. Now, thought energy has a habit of collecting or attracting like kind, as I would explain. Did you know that places have concentrations or clouds of thought energy of like kind? Have you ever seen an unfriendly place?

*"Yes, I have."*

Would you feel unfriendly in this place?

*"Definitely."*

If you were to stay there, your degree of friendliness, as a friendly being, might be affected. Is this not so?

*"Yes."*

By this, I mean that if you stayed there for any length of time, you would then have to adjust or change from the way you were or face adversity. The obvious choice would be not to stay. But there would be another choice, wouldn't there, if one were free to make it? Joe 2 would not have this problem, would he? Joe 2 would be evolved enough in his direction of thought to clearly make the choice of where he chose to live, not reacting one way or the other. Joe 2 would be living, then, from a lighter or loftier level which brings freedom. So you see, you can also "order" whiter, lighter or brighter thought and you can live from that level. This goes on, then, to say that all energy would then respond to a level of thought. If one were evolved to a bright enough level, then there would be no barrier of resistance, which is time, and no confusion. This, you would say, is closer to oneness or clear mindedness or brightness.

Now, if one were living where I live, then a thought instantly manifests a scene or an object etherically since time is not a factor. One can evolve to the level of thought where this then becomes possible in the physical universe. Now, you might say, by virtue of this channel, my thought becomes a physical thing and, indeed, it does. Clearly, there are no insurmountable barriers to the process. Now, maybe you might ask me something and I could become the universal intercessor interpreting your thought process and helping it into manifestation. This book would be such an example. In ways that would be difficult to describe, the printing of this book is arranged in this manner, carrying it into solid form.

Now, one is bombarded constantly by waves of energy, most of them undetected by your conscious receptors. Imagine, then, that you are surrounded by clouds of energy, both those of thought and energy, which by now we have discovered have a degree of intelligence. What order in this cloud would your conscious receptors understand?

*"What are conscious receptors?"*

Well, I didn't wish you to go to sleep on the job, obviously. I'm glad you asked. It is obvious that sight and hearing, smell, taste and touch enter into it. I speak of the physical senses, do I not? Now, each one would be backed up by at least an additional five, wouldn't it? I say at least because there is at least another level, isn't there, that which comes from within? Let us take "feel" for instance. I feel the wall. I feel it is there, its temperature, whether it is solid or not and its texture. Now, what if there was no light and you were a foot away from the wall? Would you feel it? What would you think?

*"I don't know whether I feel it or not."*

What about a bedroom that you are familiar with, in the darkness?

*"I know the layout and I can sense where to walk."*

Then you do have another sort of feeling, a feeling sense. I wonder what else you could feel with this sense.

*"I can feel lots of things: The energy of towns, houses, people, animals, moods."*

So, there is a receptor within you that would determine the energy of both physical and nonphysical objects, isn't that so?

*"Yes."*

If one can then hone this sense by raising his vibration in some way, then one would sense more, couldn't he?

(Seth conducts an experiment.)

I am holding this stone which I will use as a transfer point to illustrate raising your energy for the purposes of this experiment. Now, you don't exactly know when I am doing this, but in a moment, you will see what I mean.

Now, did you feel it or see it?

*"I saw it."*

What was it that you saw?

*"I was looking out the window at the yard and the yard became brighter."*

Did it coincidentally have any tinge of color to it?

*"I saw a white cloud form in the center of the yard."*

This would be indicative of a higher, brighter vibration, wouldn't it? This has some meaning when it comes to everyday life. If one is in a low mood, then the external looks darker. If one is in a higher mood, then the external looks brighter. Do you see the effect, then, on many beings of dark, cloudy or rainy days?

*"I'm a little confused. The day is not bright. When you raised my vibrations, it appeared to be brighter. But who's affecting who? Did my vibration level or mood change the degree of brightness?"*

Here is the way it works. In the absence of any directed effort to raise vibrations, the mood is dictated by the outside force, in this case, the weather. By raising your vibration, I assisted you in controlling your mood or changing the brightness that you perceive. In effect, what was accomplished was both were changed, the mood and the weather. Do you see this? To a small degree, you have seen but a glimpse of what is possible by changing your own influence. By changing your own influence, you then change your perception of the outer. If you would continue in this manner, you can see the possibility of controlling your own environment. By controlling your own environment, you would then have the capacity to change your moods without any influence whatsoever from outer effects. By learning this, you could be happy on cloudy, rainy days as well as beautiful sunny days. To carry this further, you could rise above all external influence. Does a question come to mind?

*"How do we do this ourselves?"*

That, indeed, is the essence of this book.

# CHAPTER 2

## USE OF THOUGHT

It is obvious by now that much random energy is available all around us. Some of this energy is thought energy, as we would know it. That is, things we would think of and are familiar with. We are familiar with a wide variety of things or concepts that would be in our experience as beings. We measure new experience as new thought. We use thought in nearly an unlimited fashion. That is, at times it is limited by the conscious mind and at times the mind opens to the greater self, allowing in the unlimited or timeless part.

Now, there is a concept that I wish to entertain at this time. This would be a particular use of the thought process. We have already seen how thought is chained together in a way sometimes disconcerting to a given being. One thing leads to another and to another and right back to the beginning, but with the opposite conclusion. Obviously, this chain is like a record and this use or misuse is not constructive. One would start with a thought, then, and end with its opposite. Confusion then results, leaving the being in a "non-state" of mind. If one really thought about it, one might think he was "crazy." Now, if you would interpret the word "crazy," you might look at it as meandering in a directionless fashion. This would be my definition for this particular idea. This becomes a pattern or *cycle*.

Now, what I shall discuss here are cycles of thought. Beings get into cycles that are underneath the surface that clearly rule or drive their lives. Sometimes, beings realize that they are in these cycles near the end of them and would give up in a state of despair, stating there is no way to break the cycle. Addiction, such as alcoholism, could be categorized as a cycle. There are different cycles with different alcoholics, but unless the cycle is broken, it clearly leads to their demise. There are other cycles, such as an anger cycle, which would be equally destructive, leading to dismemberment, disease and again, demise. Each cycle could then be stronger and stronger until it reaches its destructive stage. As this cycle gets stronger and stronger, there need be some form of release, or it would be like an out of control, spinning device which eventually would disentegrate. Now, so far I have talked of individual cycles only.

As you might suspect, each being would have a number of interrelated cycles. Can we use you as an example?

"*Sure.*"

All right. You have three strong cycles, don't you?

"*Yes, I do.*"

They are the alternate cycles of defiance, withdrawal and love or affection. In the love state, all is wonderful, characterized by high energy. Very little bothers you. Much is accomplished with little effort. This might coincide with the state of being. Is this true?

"*Very true.*"

This state is also one of good mood and light coloration. Of course, you would not know about the coloration, but I believe that at this time, you suspect something. Brighter day, isn't it?

"*Yes, it is.*"

The love state is the most efficient state and being a higher state, requires little energy. Thoughts in this state are manifested quite easily and with but little effort. All things in this state are not difficult to let go of, for you see, being at a loftier level, it is difficult for negative thought to reach you. Yes, indeed, you go up and down your scale or what I would call your sphere, in a manner that you do not suspect. Your great teachers are in the love state.

Now, one could give this message to beings and what do you think they would do with it?

"*They would wonder how to be in the love state all of the time.*"

That's what I thought. If one is in this state, then it is very easy for him to accept it. However, if one is not in this state, it is foreign to him.

Now, let us take another part of your cycle. The defiant state is one you would not recognize now, would you.

*"No, it seems remote."*

It is lower in vibration, where you are not now. This is a "control" state that is generally quite active with a lot of energy, little thought and not much direction. You might call it your "house cleaning mode." This is the avoidance mechanism where you would replace one sort of behavior requiring little energy with another requiring a lot of energy. You will notice that in this state, a lot of motion produces little gain. Have you noticed this?

*"Yes."*

This mode or cycle is of lower vibration and allows in other conflicting thoughts such as resentment, anger and frustration. All of these are drags on your energy. This is the state, also, where if John asked you to get some wood, it would anger you. What if he asked you to get some wood today?

*"We'd get some wood. No problem."*

All right. The defiant cycle ran its course, exhausting you. So much energy was put forth that it clearly wore you out. requiring much sleep.

What would happen next?

*"The withdrawal cycle."*

This is clearly the lowest vibrational state. Here, all things are heavy. Everything is an irritation. Conservation of energy is the foremost concern. A withdrawal would cause you to sleep many extra hours. Upon awakening, you would be still tired, lacking in energy and having little interest in anything but vegetating. If the phone rang, you would not wish to answer it. Anything that in the other modes would be joyous, would be of little interest to you here. Life becomes such a slow, heavy, plodding, mundane existence that it would be bothersome to breathe. Do you recognize this state now?

*"Yes, unfortunately."*

If vibrations could be measured, the higher number being larger and the lower number being smaller on a scale, your love state would be a three, your defiant state a two and your withdrawal state a less-than-one. One of the more interesting aspects of this is that this is not a straight line ascension. In the lower mode, and realize that there are no lines clearly separating them, your capacity or potential for intelligent, light thought is as the base of an inverted pyramid, little area for thought. The next mode up as you ascend the inverted pyramid, has a much greater area. The third mode up does not have a top on it and is expansive in area. You might even say it is unlimited. The higher mode thought has much greater velocity.

Again, most beings have cycles. We used you as but an illustration of types of thought cycles that control beings. The inverted pyramid, of course, is but an illustration. In actuality, it is an ever-expanding, upward spiral. Each time you travel around the spiral or increase vibrations, you wind up at a higher level.

Now, these cycles could vary in length, dependent upon the relative evolution or vibration of the being in question. As one raises one's vibrations by whatever means, the cycle becomes shorter and shorter in duration. Eventually, the cycles become as one. In other words, they merge. It would be interesting to view a being walking toward you who had evolved to rapid cycling. You might say, "Which one do I get, the defiant, affectionate or withdrawn one?" Fortunately, by this time, the being generally realizes which state he is in. It is possible, of course, as I will illustrate later on in this book, to step up and step out of an undesired cycle.

Before getting to those techniques, however, it is important to discuss some others on the way. Many have spoken of using a thought to create a cloud of white light around themselves for protection from lower vibrational influences or heavy energy. How does this work? What does this mean?

*"I'm glad this is coming up. I've heard it, I've done it, it works, but I don't know how."*

Oh, I'm glad you asked. What is white light? It is but God energy, of course. Would you like a little God energy?

*"Of course."*

As I suggested previously, the thought is put out and let go of. But this thought is a little different in that it directly goes to code or to color. Instead of asking God for help on this, you intercede in a more direct fashion by asking specifically for God to provide,

God being the universe, His personal cloud of protection. It is said like this (humorously), "God, your color, please." (Seth motions toward the ceiling.) The universe then says, "All right, you're covered with it." By asking specifically, directly, one timelessly receives the energy needed for protection.

Now, maybe it isn't the "knight in shining armor," but the knight with a shield of white. White and black thought do not mutually attract and the higher succeeds in warding off the lower. Do you understand this?

"*Yes.*"

If there is a white cloud, might there be another?

"*There might be a purple one for when you don't want to go so far.*"

That is excellent. But this is a little different variety than you might think. Expressing the desire to be surrounded by such a cloud brings one to a state of restfulness and well-being. It is a supporting, billowing, massaging, directed mass employing what many would know as grace to assuage their discomforting thought. It is a special form of permeating spiritual energy, carrying one in a manner that he cannot carry himself. Do you understand?

"*Of course.*"

All right. On to the next mechanism. You and John have a special friend who would come up with ideas on controlling thought. I like this one especially because beings will use it and that makes it desirable. The more than ordinary idea behind this one that makes it appealing is that it uses thought energy to control thought. I won't tell you why, but it just works. Now, your friend would say, "Imagine a round screen with an electrical wire attached to it which leads to a very large lever that you can pull or throw. Would you pull it or throw it?"

"*Neither. I would push it.*"

Clever. When a thought that you do not want starts to penetrate, you push the lever, engaging the mechanism which electrifies the screen, putting out an energy that attracts and collects the thought. This stops the thought from entering for all time. If one would use this and another technique from the same friend, it would be but a short time for the concept or level of your thought to be lighter and brighter. Let us call this the etheric thought screen, a way of using thought to create a device for controlling the input of thought you don't want, both from yourself and from other sources.

Now, let us discuss the other technique suggested by your friend that would root out unwanted, stored thought which just might be behind your unwanted cycle. Imagine a thick mass boiling in a pool. Within the mass are floating certain round objects. Now, the mass is not hot to the touch. You have surfaced a thought of discontent that you do not want. Reach into the pool and pull out the offending thought, cut it off with a scissors and then cut it in half.

This concept can provide an interesting proof of its inner workings. If it is used enough, it will be but a short time and half thoughts will start coming out, providing the thinker with an interesting dilemma. The dilemma is this: When the half thought is presented, then it becomes obvious there is a choice. The choice is this: Does one want to continue with the behavior or change it? The beauty of this particular technique is that it not only takes into account thought to pull thought, but it also particularly would be palatable to the ego, which likes action. When the ego actually sees what is going on and approves of it, you can rest assured the change will be quite rapid. The first technique, of course, also takes the ego into account by enlisting its aid in telling itself how clever it is to be able to create such a machine to help *save* itself.

Now, some other uses of thought are for affirming something, generating ideas, changing something, constructing and communicating. When you affirm something, what do you do? Do you know?

*"I have never felt inclined to do affirmations. I suppose it would be a step toward manifesting. I feel strongly that affirmations are not the way for me. My whole thrust has been to find God's will for me and that does not include affirming a thought that I might think would be the best for me. I have no doubt that I could manifest through affirmations, but do I really know what is the best for me?"*

So the reason you wouldn't use affirmations is not by personal preference, but because of fear of unwanted results. Now, what if I had a way of adding to without fear of subtracting from? Would you be interested?

*"If it's a guarantee, I would."*

You are cautious, aren't you? All right, I guarantee it. Let us say that a desire comes to mind. Let us say the aforementioned new car. One needs to get specific about one's needs, such as the approximate size, usefulness, efficiency and mechanical condition. One can then write it down, picture it, feel it or affirm with a combination of these. So far, so good, right?

*"Right."*

So far, this is a subject of many books and I will not go into detail from here. What would one need to be, so that the fear part would not enter the picture?

*"Confident that what you affirmed was the best for you."*

But you wanted a guarantee, did you not?

*"Yes."*

Now, if this would be followed by the words, "I trust that the result of this affirmation or affirmations is in accordance with the highest good (love) for me," I have given you a guarantee, have I not?

*"Yes, that feels right."*

Now, what have I done here? I have released it in trust of universal intelligence which would allow trust in this process to work out what is best for me. In other words, I have released the thought (let go) in love. It could be anything, for all you have done is affirm, if it is best for me, then I will leave the rest up to the universe. Is it clear on affirmations?

*"Yes."*

Do you think you would ever use them?

*"Yes."*

All right. Thought is used to generate ideas. Let us say a need arises and the seed then is planted. Does anything come to mind? Now, let us say that there was a need to remove grass in an area difficult to reach. After exploring what was available, nothing was found to suit the need. One then becomes stopped and the thought comes, "I need something that will fill this need." The thinker then would go on to something else. It might be an idle thought or one with heavy concentration. The universe then takes this thought and attempts to fill the need. In the mail comes a magazine advertising a new left-handed ground gouger.

It just happens to fulfill your need. It will gouge the ground in just the right way. You might think, "What a coincidence. How could this happen?" But there are no coincidences, you see, just coincident thought. Surprisingly, this might occur a day prior to the need or on the very day of the need. It would seem that something or someone was reading your mind. When one truly lets go of a thought, even idle ones would come into fruition. Now, sometimes the idle ones are faster than the directed ones because nothing is attached to them. The velocity of the thought is directly proportional to the degree that any attachment is then let go. The most rapid thought is then the one which has no attachment. This is not an easy area for beings. Since most thought is multiple without the thinker knowing, it thus becomes a challenge to the thinker to detach any riders to the thought. Does this seem easy to you?

*"No, it doesn't."*

(Johnny and Mia, our token teenagers, come home from school for lunch. Seth asks Mia if she can come up with a single unattached thought. Mia says, "I saw a certain black sports car." Seth asks, "Is there any thought attached to it?" Mia replies, "I need to get gas and oil for it." Mia then says, "This is not so easy." Seth asks Johnny the same question. Johnny replies, "I see a picture of me driving a sports car on La Jolla Boulevard with my sun glasses on." Seth then asks Johnny if there was any succeeding thought. Johnny says, "I see my mansion, also." Seth then asks him if there was any blank space after the first thought and Johnny says, "What do you mean?" Mia and Johnny then leave to return to school.)

Now, do you think this is easy? Has there been any time when you have been successful?

*"Yes, at times of desperation."*

Why would this have been succesful?

*"Because I completely let go of the results and there was a blank space afterward. The letting go came because I had no more answers."*

Now, let us take two examples. One, thought can generate pictures or feelings that help you manifest the outcome. Your sphere of consciousness, as I call it, has the capability to generate a blueprint of thought which creates a picture of the pattern or thought to be created. This could be for any material object or for something else, depending upon what is needed. The picture of an object, whether it be complete or under construction, helps generate the energy needed to complete it. Secondly, the thought is generated that would enable the universe to fill in the blanks. So, in essence, thought generates thought or a chain which orders, in two senses, the manifestation. First, it is ordered in sequence and then by energy.

Hopefully, this is not too confusing. In essence, maybe several pictures might be involved for something under construction, whereas an object such as a car would be completed by the involvement of a number of other intersecting events that the mind would not picture.

Now, here comes an idea that would complete a picture of an action that you need which is not easily pictured. Let us say, for purposes of this discussion, that you were tired of defiant behavior. How would you change this? Do you know?

*"No."*

First, you could ask a friendly psychologist or psychiatrist. In lieu of this, you could ask for help. Do you know what I mean?

*"Pray. Ask God to remove the behavior because everything I've tried hasn't worked."*

What happened?

*"The behavior was removed. It is no longer a problem."*

How?

*"A sequence of events occurred which exposed the behavior so glaringly that I became very aware of it."*

Now, what actually transpired when you asked was the creation of an etheric energy device which led in directed energy in a fashion which exposed John's behavior to him as a trigger for your behavior. Unknown to him, he was acting as a trigger and you would react in a defiant way. All of a sudden, John became aware that the way he was saying something had charged energy behind it in a way that would trigger you. This opened the cycle in John which would generate unwarranted expectations of you causing you to act defiantly. This thought-prayer of yours, with the blank space behind it of no thought, caused the universe to generate in the most efficient manner this etheric device which would bring out John's behavior.

I like this example because it serves to illustrate how powerful thought really is. Your thought actually created an intelligent energy bank that by its very presence would not allow the behavior to continue, with the permission of both of you.

This would seem to illustrate that the universe would go to any lengths to complete thought. This energetic device could also be thought of as a communication transformer. A discordant thought would go out and would be re-routed or bent in a way that would cause the sender to review the thought prior to or at the beginning of a new cycle. You might even look at it as a random thought processor. It could also be thought of as a filter for cleaning up your thought. Another example of a thought system would be the ordered generation of music. By sitting down at an instrument, let us say, and opening yourself up or, in essence, creating a void, one would allow the generation of "new" music. This can be done with or without musical talent. Usually, it is along the lines of a talent already possessed, for this would form the attraction. The universe would see this void that needed to be filled. Now, if the receiver was truly open, any kind of music could flow in. If the receiver had some preconceived idea of the type of music, then it would be along this line. The creation of an unlimited supply of music is then available. Since the new music is created in a timeless fashion, all that ever was or will be is available. The term, "all is available," not only applies to music, but to everything else.

Now, let us suppose that one did not have a preconceived need. If one then would let go and open up, a constant succession of ideas would filter in. What would this individual be called?

*"A genius."*

Yes, a genius or an inventor. Then the question comes to mind, "What is intelligence?" Is intelligence defined in the sense of your conscious ability or is it what you are able to bring in or is it what you are able to store?

*"All of it."*

Indeed it is and more. Now, how would you measure it?

*"You couldn't measure it."*

That is true. There are tests which would seek to measure intelligence in more than one way, but a number of factors are not taken into account and the tests fail miserably. For what do they attempt to measure? That is what I do not understand. First of all, one has to understand what intelligence is and where it comes from before designing a method of measurement. Who is intelligent?

*"Everybody and everything."*

That is true. But, when one refers to someone as "being intelligent," what does he mean?

*"Someone he thinks knows more than he does."*

That's brilliant. That must mean you're intelligent, because you think as I do. It is a measure of relativity, isn't it? Now, would an engineer be regarded as intelligent if in two areas of his life, engineering and mathematics, he is superior to the average?

*"Yes."*

Would another engineer, who was superior to most in the same areas, but in addition, was accomplished in music and investments, regard the first engineer as intelligent?

*"Not particularly."*

Here is one of the most destructive areas or ideas or patterns of thought used by beings. They would compare their capability with others without living in the other's consciousness. This is so destructive that it has wasted many incarnations. A comparison with an artificial standard can lead to a lessening of confidence, ablity and a feeling of depression.

Now, let us examine what takes place here. Have you ever felt less than another?

*"Many times."*

Name one.

*"Once, at a party, I was engaged in conversation with a psychiatrist, a newspaper editor and an U.S. ambassador. The thought suddenly struck me, emblazoned in red, 'What am I doing in this conversation? I don't belong here. I feel less than.' The party was ruined for me."*

Notice you thought it in indelible red. This was to set the emotional charge to beat yourself down to the point that you might not think well of yourself again. Now, many could identify with this unfortunate position that you did to yourself. You thought that they thought, therefore, you thought. Is that right?

*"Yes. I remember feeling afraid that they would find out."*

What were you afraid of? What would they find out?

*"That I was not as knowledgeable, as educated, as smart as they were. I felt that I was faking it."*

By which standard did you measure yourself? You can't answer, can you?

*"No, I can't."*

Because there is no answer. Did you know that?

*"No."*

So, you beat yourself up for no reason. How many times has this happened to beings, causing them so much unnecessary suffering? Now, let us try to understand the essence of intelligence. First of all, it would depend on the mode or mood of thought you are in, in the now moment. If you are happy, you are confident, you are of a higher vibration, higher energy and are of higher intelligence. Secondly, it is the degree of your evolvement that would give you access to greater intelligence. The condition of your emotional or mental health, which also coincides with your physical health, be it up or down, is a contributing factor in your access to information. Another factor might enable one to "channel" information in various modes that would access them to greater intelligence. It has long been thought that intelligence was of the brain, but in actuality, it is of the conscious mind, which I call the sphere. The more conscious one becomes, the greater the access to information.

There are cases where the brain, the transfer unit to the physical world from consciousness, was damaged in much of the area thought to contain intelligence. In some of these cases, these beings apparently had no lack of knowledge. Now, who is superior and who is inferior? That is the question, isn't it?

*"No one is superior or inferior. I say that, but sometimes slip into feeling inferior."*

Then it would be a matter of "feeling good" about yourself, wouldn't it? The quickest way, if you are in a low mood, would be to elevate your consciousness. One of the ways to accomplish this is to concentrate on one of your areas of abilities which would help you to begin to feel good about yourself. John does this when playing the piano, doesn't he?

*"Yes."*

He lets the music flow through him to heighten his sense of awareness. Another way is to elevate yourself to the love state, clearly superior to all others. At this level, much more intelligence is available to everyone. There are those rare beings who are in this state constantly. Who are they?

*"The masters."*

That is true. These are the beings who have mastered their egos and therefore, have no interference from realizing higher intelligence. What is the ego?

*"The false personality we create in order to survive here."*

Yes. The ego is a system of colorations or hues and feelings designed as filters to ward off or protect from what one would regard as an evil world. When one is incarnated, one necessarily brings in some ego due to the influence of entering a time and space block. Some masters here for service would be of such a fine vibration that it would have little or no influence over them. They know what the ego is and would seek to rise above it. It still would be but little effort on their part to be engaged again in the games of the ego and they would need to be vigilant to negate its false influence. Its false influence, of course, is the cyclical nature that I have already explained. Yes, even the masters are subject to the temptations that one hears of Satan or the ego. Much has been written of the ego. From the point of view of the ego, it generally escapes what is true and real by turning it around as a defense and making everything upside down and backwards. It literally turns its back on thought and would seek to find the quickest available hiding place for it.

Now, what does the ego do when it finds a situation that it cannot deal with?

*"Depends on the situation."*

Yes. When it is flattered, it would take the flattery and seek to bolster itself for having done a good job, even though it may not know who was responsible for the credit it is taking. The ego is rather small, relatively, in the overall area of the sphere or mind. If a threat is presented to the body, known as the ego, then it would react in the same manner that it would believe others would react to it. That is, it would believe, since it wishes and knows destruction, that others would destroy it. When the ego gets cornered and threatened, it soon becomes overwhelmed and then finds that it has but few alternatives from which to draw. By its very nature, it is necessarily limited. When thought is contained within the limited ego structure, it is of a closed variety. By this, I mean it knows not where to go for help. When it is confronted with a situation in which it knows not how to deal in its limited capacity, it would go into the fight or flight mode. Not knowing how to deal with many situations, it would then file them in what you know as the subconscious, believing that it would deal with them later. The problem with the ego is that later never comes and a rather large stored problem area begins to develop as one regresses to childhood. The ego's method of dealing with a situation would be to match it with something that happened before. The danger inherent in this is that no two situations are exactly alike. When one starts awakening and using higher thought, each new situation is then dealt with as something as it is, new. This is when the greater intelligence comes into play.

The ego, with its fight or flight tendency, is a lower vibrational influence using reactive thought, sometimes automatically, instead of higher "reason" to solve problems. Many beings, after discovering the problems inherent with using the ego, become angry with it and would seek to destroy it. This, in effect, is playing the ego's game, for it seeks destruction also. The ultimate goal of the ego, being insane, of course, is suicide. The seeker of higher truth would be better served in seeking ways to retrain the ego. How would one do this?

*"Convince it in a way that it would understand."*

Yes. You would flatter it, informing it that its clever ways have found a more intelligent way of solving problems. This must be done in such a way that the ego does not feel threatened. Being false, the ego would not know truth if it struck it in the face. Being backward, one needs to bring truth through the back door, so as to speak. By telling it how clever it is or having it use cleverness to keep itself busy, one then slips in truth so that it becomes part of the structure.

Now, the structure is such that there is no clear line of demarcation from the ego to the greater self or soul. There is a gray area in which there is a mixture of both. When one raises one's vibrations to higher intelligence, then one seeks to use a larger and larger part of the gray area.

When one begins to release the ego and use a larger and larger proportion of the sphere, other feelings would then come in. These feelings would enable one to pick up the level of other beings and assess what they are dealing with. One hears of reading auras. What does this mean? Do you know?

*"Looking at the color or colors surrounding a person's body gives me an idea of what mode or mood they are in."*

Now, not all process colors in the "seeing" mode. Some process colors in the "feeling" mode. Other use of internal senses may also come into play. Some of these may trigger abilities from other incarnations. Did you know that?

*"I suspected it."*

After a little aside, let us get back to our discussion of intelligence. One suddenly thinks that he is a writer, a painter or perhaps a sculptor. Why would one suddenly start thinking this?

*"Because they've done it before in another incarnation. That is misleading, since all incarnations are happening simultaneously, so I'll say that it is because they are open to using universal intelligence."*

When one follows one's "calling," one is, indeed, where he would be the most happy. This might change from time to time, when the soul suddenly decides that it would like other experience and then in comes the thought, "Why don't we try something else?"

This channel, John, happens to be one of those. Due to his particular bank of experiences in other incarnations, including channeling, John is a bit more versatile than most in changing direction when the calling comes in. Hopefully, he doesn't change direction until this book is finished.

All of this could be and need be categorized as intelligence. Now, after all of that, can you now tell me how to measure intelligence?

*"No way."*

Now, would you see any way that the average, reasonable being, knowing all of this, could ever feel less than?

*"No. I have a lot of abilities that others don't have and others have a lot of abilities that I don't have. All it means is that we can gain a whole lot more if we focus on what we can add to each other. We all have what we need for growth this time around."*

It is of no small importance for those who would seek to use their abilities to find that they quickly form into focus and it is with ease that their understanding and being arrives. Someone might say, "I wish to be a painter," but in effect, painters starve. If one strongly wishes to become a painter, then the universe wishes him to become a painter and he will not starve. In other words, the strongest thought comes through in the form of a calling and puts forth other chained programs or directions that would automatically have this come about. Little or no effort need be made by the painter and in no time, the paint is flowing. Now, it is known that truly great paintings are inspired by depths of color and feeling that do not seem to be of this world. Obviously, the calling of these painters is so strong that universal intelligence will see that these abilities are allowed to be spread.

Now, many beings become stagnated in their vocations and become dull, boring and lifeless. When something becomes boring and there is no interest, clearly the universe is telling you that something new and fresh need be looked at. This can be a new attitude, a new way of looking at something, a new direction, a new occupation, or all of these. Let us take the secretary in an office who is tired of typing. The difficulty is, the ego says that she is not intelligent, relatively, and is stuck in her present occupation. Many beings spend years in this dilemma because they are listening to false information. What would you do if this were the case in your life?

*"Marry a channel!"*

All right then. You've got me this time. That is indeed one way out, but they are a little hard to find.

*"Not if you send out a white. thought!"*

You have the right idea. One is never really stuck without reason for learning. When one would find oneself in such a position, one need stand back and let go, asking for universal intelligence to fill in the blanks. Then, in a way that you probably would never think of, a change in direction would come about.

# CHAPTER 3

## VARIABLES OF THOUGHT

What is a thought variable? Have you any idea?

*"None."*

A thought variable is a thought that would be the same, but would be relegated to more than one level, due to its emotional charge and would be colored accordingly. Have you ever heard of a black thought?

*"I've not only heard of them, I've had them."*

An angry, depressing or vengeful thought might be referred to as a black thought.

(Seth gets up and shows us a dance from his Russian incarnation. No one pays much attention and he says, "Well, maybe that was one of my more boring incarnations.")

I only wished to explain that the weight of the foot and the leg was used to propel themselves around.

*"I apologize for ignoring you."*

That will do. Now, that thought could be any number of things. One could be angry at being ignored and one could choose to ignore the ignorer. This would be maybe an orange thought, a medium variety ego thought stored with this hue upon it. Now, let us say that the ignored one then encountered another situation whereby he applied for a new position that was quite important to him. He had studied long and hard and could only work with this one particular company. Within this company, he needed to see only one individual. This particular individual was *the* decision maker. Now, the decision maker chose to ignore our friend in a most blatant, insulting, obnoxious manner and slammed the door in his face. This was a shock to our friend. He didn't know what to do. Powerful emotions filled him and thoughts of revenge and mayhem were engendered. Now, these were stored in a nearly black mode. Our friend eventually resolved the situation by finding a like kind of job with a more friendly place of employment.

The problem with this experience is that it was stored and not dealt with. Our friend much later encountered a being who, in conversation with others, didn't hear our friend's question and did not respond. In other words, our friend thought he was being ignored. A violent reaction was triggered from our friend and he had to be escorted away from the room where the conversation took place. This particular conversation took place years after he was ignored by the decision maker on the job for which he had applied. Why do you think this particular outburst was triggered?

*"I don't know."*

I know you don't know. For our simplistic example, there were two thoughts that were buried with charge but along the some line of being ignored. Why would one be triggered and not the other?

*"Maybe the friend who ignored him looked like the decision maker."*

Indeed. That is exactly correct. You "guess" well.

*"That was not a "guess," Seth. I told you I was sorry for ignoring your dancing."*

Now, it could be that the black thought was triggered by a particular movement, clothes, room, table or even a similar plate or other utensil that might have been in the same room as the incident of the black thought. Now, the black thoughts are stored in the lower vibrational area of the sphere coded in a manner that would be close to the fight or flight reaction area. You might think of this as the cave man syndrome: Hit them with the club or run.

Now, our friend could have had the milder ignored thought triggered if the association had been coded to something familiar with this particular orange area. We have only discussed here two variables, when in effect, there might be one hundred stored variables. Unfortunately, for our friend, the more violent one or out of control variable was associated or struck.

Now, already I have opened a huge potential for action or reaction from these examples. Obviously, these variables are reached by some process and this is of coded association. If one had access to these codes, then one could reach nearly anything stored by any being, provided one was willing to test the water. Imagine layer upon layer of stored thought. Each layer would be in various hues of color, according to its emotional charge. Each thought, then, would have a trigger or triggers. They would be categorized by events, time, place, objects, colors and a variety of other things placed there in some order. The poor, unsuspecting creature known as a being, who would be attached to this very expansive mass, would be at the mercy of its beck and call.

Naturally, along with this, some form of control would need be implaced to allow the unsuspecting being to exist in the physical world. Let us go back to our friend, again, with his black reaction. There was no control placed around the trigger of this entrenched thought. A "normal" being would have placed a controlling thought around the emotionally charged thought or event, preventing an embarrasing or violent reaction, allowing him to live in society.

This controlling thought would be stored along the chain by experience and would prevent or filter out, in most cases, the over-reaction. How do you restrain yourself?

*"By learned behavior."*

Somewhere a block is placed in front of the emotionally charged thought, which is useful in controlling the reaction in most cases. So, we have a control mechanism in most beings. This would be another thought variable. In other words, we have the thought and the controlling thought. So far, so good. There is a problem, however. This controlling mechanism can short-circuit at times and would seek to control behavior in a manner that need not be controlled. Let us say that someone takes advantage of us. We learned at some time in our past that when a situation of this type arises, our over-violent reaction to it gets us into a lot of difficulty. This capacity in beings, to short-circuit, causes a type of behavior that can lead to great stress. That is, if one would seek to control a violent reaction and not succeed, as our friend did not succeed, then the next situation similar to it would be over-controlled. This is where the problem with the short-circuiting comes in. When one seeks to over-control, too much emphasis is then placed on control. That is, so much charge is put on the thought, more than is needed, that it causes the controlling block to leak over into another block of thoughts and influence behavior in another area. What is an area in which you might find yourself out of control?

*"Withdrawal. First I feel angry, stuff it and then go into withdrawal."*

Now, you over-control anger and it leaks over and forces withdrawal. Do you understand this?

*"Yes."*

What would happen if you had a way of reducing the charge of that variable?

*"I would use it because I no longer enjoy withdrawal."*

What might you think would be the result of reducing the power of that variable?

*"I think I would get angry, express my feelings and not go into withdrawal."*

Indeed, you have over-compensated, fearing out of control anger and it then bleeds over into withdrawal. The problem with over-compensating is that many other areas of behavior are affected in ways that you would not suspect. To control an area of behavior that is frightening results in extra charge being placed which throws one out of balance. This lack of balance can result in a controlling mechanism that can rest in place for an extended period of time, sometimes a lifetime.

Now, let us say that we have a friend, Bruce, who would realize that something is driving him that he does not understand. In several areas of his life, he would find that some other part of him takes over and causes him to act without realizing where the impetus comes from. Bruce does not know from where the problem stems. He only suspects it because in many areas of his life he acts in an irrational manner. He has a problem of getting some place on time. He has difficulty if anyone tells him what to do. He has difficulty if anyone becomes too close or too emotional. This would cause Bruce to withdraw or wish to run and hide. This sometimes comes out at the most inopportune times. Bruce has failed in every area in his attempts to uncloud this issue.

Bruce decides that the only way out of this is with some kind of divine help. So Bruce says a white thought prayer and releases it. What do you think happens?

*"His white thought prayer brings immediate action."*

Now, in this case, permission was given to the universe to generate a form of energy that would go into a place which would activate the out of control control variable. Sounds like a play on words, doesn't it? In this case, it just so happens that I became directly involved. There is an area which I can see and if you were properly attuned, you could see, also, that contained the problem area. I used something that you might say is a magic wand. The magic wand in this case was one half of a set of divining rods. I merely floated energy into the affected area stimulating it to the surface of the conscious mind. Out rushed all of this emotion that had been hidden for many years. It was interesting for Bruce to see just how many areas of his life were affected by this one variable. All of a sudden, Bruce finds himself free to express his feelings and/or emotions. The gamut of feelings is run. The mother of all fear is resurrected and depression could result unless Bruce becomes aware of what it is that he has brought forth.

What has Bruce brought forth? Bruce has released a heavier, negative emotion that was dragging him down. Happily for Bruce, who doesn't now realize who he is, this period doesn't last long. Now Bruce still is all of that which he was, plus. He does not have the burden of the heavy energy dragging him down. Bruce is now a lighter, brighter being. Bruce truly becomes who he is. Bruce is then a collection of freer, what you might call nicer thoughts, bringing him to the level where he, for the first time, is free to express his wants and needs. Do you understand this?

*"Yes, I do."*

When I said Bruce is still who he was, plus, that meant Bruce is the brighter collection of thoughts, not restricted by the heavy emotional charge that would keep him from expressing.

Bruce's prayer literally brought me into the picture and it could have been in many ways and caused me to energize the affected area. This example would point out some of the effects of an out of control control variable. When control variables are in place, working in a desired manner, they only have sufficient charge to control the one area of thought that they were designated to control. For instance, an angry thought would have a control variable which would restrict the anger from running away, causing a disproportionate amount of damage than the stimulus would call for. Once a control variable which has been a problem is corrected in any manner, the uplifting freedom cannot help but bring out the higher, finer thoughts of the being in question.

Now, let us discuss another variable. This would be a connecting variable, the variable that connects one thought with another. This variable is put in place, let us say, when a new thought comes in, not readily able to connect to any previous thought in the sphere. These variables also have a code and the code is then attached to the thought in question. Let us take the words New-Age and pretend that the individual in question had never heard this term. The thought would be implanted and a connecting variable with a code word attached to it. The thought in the sphere would then "lie" there with the amount of charge and what we will call nuance placed on it until it is again needed.

Now, let us say that the word "thought" was the code for this particular area. This is unlikely, but for purposes of this idea, we'll use it. So if someone says the word "thought" and it immediately strikes the chord of New-Age, then the connecting variable is triggered and all connected would be brought out. All of the feelings then associated with the implantation of this thought would be brought forth unless something threatening was placed there with it. Then a control variable or block might be also placed with it. In most cases, this does not result because the charge is not sufficient to warrant it. Now, the next time any thought comes in about New-Age, the information, complete with charge, is stored with it. Some thought is stored with so little charge that it is placed in such a remote area of the sphere that it would be difficult to access.

If a nondescript car happened to go by your house and you noticed it, unless there was any charge of sufficient nature to warrant remembering it, it would be difficult to access this thought later. All experience is stored on some level, but the charge may be so weak that under most circumstances, it would not be accessible.

Now, the sphere or mind is always active. In your sleep state, it would seek ways to work out some of the excess thought that was charged and placed there during your waking hours. The dream state works very much as the "awake" state. Thoughts are generated and they go through the chain creating images which turn out to be events. They are connected, controlled, processed, associated and created in a way that an efficient testing mode is pictured. Let us say that a situation comes up that you cannot deal with, either because of lack of information or an unresolved conflict. Your circuitry becomes overloaded. The charged thought would then be stored in an area that we'll call the variable area. Do you think these thoughts would be just processed in your dream state when you are asleep?

*"No."*

That is the correct answer. While you are walking or sitting around, going through your awake state, you are also dreaming. If you knew how to get in touch with those dreams, you would see or feel them while you're awake. Would you like to see one of these?

*"Yes, or course."*

(Seth conducts and experiment.)

Now, what I did was generate a little energy with these divining rods in an area of your sphere where a dream-awake state was being played out or worked out to release you from the bondage of feeling artificially restricted. Do you feel this?

*"I feel happier."*

Now, when you did the same thing with John, what was the result?

*"He felt freer."*

Yes, that is true, for what happened was his dream-awake state was working out his fears and discharging the heavy charge in a way that would make him lighter and freer. This goes on one hundred percent of the time, regardless of whether you are asleep or awake.

Of course, another way of contacting or intercepting what is being worked out is in the meditative state. With a little practice, you then disengage external influence and work out what is being worked on in a most efficient and expeditious manner.

If one becomes overwhelmed or overcharged, then one need

discharge it. One can discharge it by contacting the dream state in the awake state, sleeping or meditating. Now, there is a connecting variable between the lower fear thoughts and the higher unrestricted thoughts. When the variable area takes a heavy thought in a prioritized manner, the most highly charged thought causing the most trouble is then worked out in the most rapid fashion. The higher the area that the dream state can be worked out, the more efficient the process. If one primarily lived under low vibrational influence, it would take more time to work out problems necessarily than if one were under higher influence. So, if one entered the sleep state knowingly and asked to have one's dreams worked out at the white level, then their solution would be presented in a more expeditious manner.

Now, I pointed the wand at you at about the solar plexis area. I then thought a white thought and raised the wand upward, over your head. How did you feel then?

*"I felt better, more awake."*

What happened when you did the same thing to John?

*"He felt happier."*

So, when you raise your vibrations, you raise the level of your thought. When you raise the level of your thought, then it is raised to an area where greater intelligence can assist you in working out the solutions to difficulties.

Now, if you had an assistant who would raise your thought each time you encountered a difficulty, to a level offering a quicker solution, would the assistant then be valuable?

*"Very valuable."*

Now, if I ask you how much would the assistant charge you?

*"I couldn't put a price on this."*

If the assistant charged you a large sum of money each time that this would come to pass, would it be worth it?

*"I would probably decide that a new piece of furniture or a new dress would be more important."*

Now, what if the assistant was Jesus Christ?

*Long pause. "That's a whole different story. It would quickly become the top priority."*

How long would this last?

*"Until the ego resumed control."*

Now, that is being honest. For, indeed, that is what happens. If one had an unlimited number of famous assistants, then might one go on for some time being assisted out of the ego or lower vibration? Eventually, the ego would tire of the game and would seek to retake control. The ego itself then becomes a controlling variable, choosing to connect to the lower vibrational area, where it has control.

One therefore gets caught in a trap. One would stay at the level of control of the ego until the ego would become overwhelmed and would be forced to let go and reach a new level where the solution is then worked out. If one could retrain the ego to allow the assistance of its higher friends, then the trauma and drama of life in the ego would be shorter and sweeter.

Now, each connecting variable is connected in some fashion with the area you would know as the ego. Do you think that when you say you connect with someone, that this might be the way?

*"Yes."*

Yes. Their thought connects with your thought and the level of connection somewhat matches. Do you think you and John connect in thought and level?

*"Yes. If we didn't, we wouldn't be together."*

Do you think there would be any other variables?

*"I'm sure there are."*

Yes, that's true. There are color or what you would call mood variables. This places the thought at the right level. A higher thought would be directed to the higher level of the sphere. Now, there is a natural process whereby the incoming thought, regardless of where it was generated, is colored according to its charge and placed at the appropriate level. If necessary, it has a control variable and a connecting variable with it. Now, the mood variable has exactly the right shade and is attached to the incoming thought and then it would be placed. Isn't that interesting?

So now we are beginning to understand how variables are used to store thought. What is missing here? Would it be how they are accessed?

*"Yes, that's what I think."*

Most beings would believe thought is something that is randomly generated, wouldn't you think?

*"The soul probably arranges it."*

You are quite correct. Situations are arranged by the soul.

Chance meetings and thought which just happen to enter your sphere are examples of this. Now, access variables are those which search the sphere for matching energy which would coincide with the entertained thoughts. Access variables can take the form of words, pure thought or energy, color or hue and a feeling. Now, let us say that a thought is put out asking for relief from a particularly troublesome situation. All thoughts relating to this experience, unless blocked, are rapidly entertained. A feeler or variable would search or seek to attract that which would complete the thought. This variable searches both within and without which would lead the universe to "fill the order."

As this variable enters timelessness, it would then be of universal code, set out in a manner without restriction to attract any energy that would make the thought complete. An access variable then may act as energy and a thought, differentiated here to serve this example; for in essence, they would be the same or of like kind. So, in effect, we have at least two kinds of access variables, one empowered to search the universe and one empowered to search the sphere. They are of like kind, for the universe would be a sphere as well as the sphere of consciousness would be a sphere.

So, the variable would be of like kind, but with a different speed. Picture this variable traveling around your planet at infinite speed. Now, in essence, it would only travel a distance in a circular motion necessary to attract energy sufficient to complete the thought it was sent to randomly access. That is a mouthful, isn't it? Do you understand, now, what takes place?

*"Not totally."*

It is interesting with these access variables in that they make up what you would regard as your greater sphere of influence. Now, the access variable of a master would have some effect upon those in a large area, possibly one hundred miles in diameter. In other words, his access variables are light enough and fast enough they they would be accessing information in that great an area to fulfill his collection of thought. In other words, he is accessing primarily from a higher, lighter area. His variables are accessing at nearly infinite speed. He would be in touch with and accessing at infinite speed in part of his sphere. Not to be confusing, this is accomplished a greater percentage in his thought process than it is in the thought processes of his not so masterful counter-parts. Do you understand this?

*"Yes, he is at a higher, faster level of thought."*

So now he becomes a master of information.

Now, the master would not have much of a controlling variable with his ego and therefore, he is accessing information that would be directed or divinely inspired. So that, to be divine, a being must be out of control in all areas. Do you understand what it means to be out of control?

*"To be out of control means to be trusting in the universe."*

A master would put out a thought and it would be healing for some beings. He would probably take a few deep breaths, stand back, figuratively, and let go. What do you think would happen then?

*"The healing would occur."*

That is true, but it might occur in a different way than you might imagine. How would you expect it to occur?

*"Since the master let go, the universe would then be in control of the form of healing best suited to the being's needs."*

Yes, that is correct. What might happen, for instance, is a local dentist might suddenly find something wrong in a tooth and a lit-tle dental work might suddenly cure the ailment which might have appeared as an inflamed nerve in the side of the face. This might point out that when people truly let go, their good will come. The good may come from any source and from where it comes, no emphasis need be put on it. The access variable then will attract the most efficient form of healing. It might be in the person of another being or it might come from any source, such as an etheric device. Being infinitely intelligent, when one lets go of a thought, the access variable merely attracts the energy necessary to fulfill the order.

What question would come to mind about an access variable?

*"How does it work?"*

Yes, that comes to mind. Okay, then. Let us use the example of the door. You wish to access the door (open it). It might be the most efficient to walk over and open it. The next time, it might be a saving of energy, that is, more efficient, for a wind that is blow-ing to access the door since it was left slightly ajar. Now, rarely does this happen. But in actual practice, it could happen if your potential thought at a given time came from a high enough vibration. The universe, being infinitely intelligent, would infinitely know this.

Now, you had a friend arrive from Oregon. You had a problem with trust. The friend had a need to be fulfilled. What do you think happened? I'll tell you. I led you to believe that there was some space, time and distance with thought. In actuality or in reality, this is not the case, for all energy and thought know of each other. That is, the most efficient recognition is programmed without a lapse of time. Now, it is very difficult to describe what I have just said. The thought went up (and I only use up figuratively) where all is known and then the thoughts knew of each other. In other words, they accessed. The universe knew that you knew each other and had a like kind of need. The most efficient way was to bring her here in physical form, given the vibrational level of both of you. Now, the conscious mind sometimes does not know that its prayer or thought has been accessed or answered. Sometime in your long conversation with her, your thought or request was answered. Did you know this?

*"I knew something was going on, but not exactly what."*

Would this be in answer to your prayer for distrust to be removed?

*"The problem was that I forgot about the prayer. So, I didn't recognize that my prayer was being answered at the time my friend was here. I realize it now."*

Now, all energy has potential and seeks to fulfill that magnetic potential. The most likely potential is then tapped, bringing completion to the thought. So then, the highest probability of your friend's and your thoughts sought to reach their most probable potential which coincided in fact or in an event called an intersection.

Can you imagine the confusion when many beings would seek to fulfill their thoughts at the same intersection? They would all wish to go to the same place. Too many would wish to use the same airplane. The universe would sort out those most probable to have the same intersection. The cumulative need of each being for the result of that intersection would then be processed according to the weight or greatest need placed on this event by any individual being. Weighty thoughts manifest, sometimes to the detriment of those putting forth the thoughts.

Now, let us say that a being had a thought about calling a particular other being by telephone. Each time the phone was used, the being would not be there or the line was busy. What do you think has happened here?

*"The person making the telephone call didn't really want to connect with the other person."*

Yes, that is one possible scenario, but another might be that the thought patterns of the two beings would not intersect efficiently at that time. Have you ever called someone, thinking something would happen of a friendly nature and the opposite occurred?

*"Yes."*

If the line was busy, literally and figuratively, it would mean either, try later without attempting to "will" your way as in self or forget about it. In other words, if you had tried a number of times and it didn't seem to work and you felt compelled to continue, then there is something of nonmatching frequency of vibration or thought which would seek to tell you to let it go. If all goes smoothly and well with your efforts, then frequency of thought would match. If all is a struggle and unknowingness takes place, then thought is of a non-coordinating variety and would tell you that the most efficient path is one of letting go.

Now, I wish to get across that the difference in your sphere of influence is not one of distance, particularly. It is more in degree of subtle nuance. Your colors or hues or moods would access in your sphere of influence rather than a heavy thought particle. So, what you might say is, "Here comes Paul. He radiates widely," or, "Paul is a colorful character." Without the restrictions of time and space, then all thought knows of all thought and it is only thought that blocks other thought or all thought would then manifest.

You came up with a beautiful example when you said, "I hate so-and-so, but he isn't all bad." On some level, good old so-and-so knows that he isn't badly hated, but hated. Old so-and-so then has a thought plus a rider thought, a mixed message. It is both a blessing and sad that the universe, in this present physical incarnation, is as it should be as of this moment. If this civilization were on a higher level that could consciously receive these thoughts, then the sender would either have to be removed or change his thought, for he would not fit in. This is very interesting to follow, for until the collective thought can be raised or cleared, then individual thought must be more specific. In other words, the disorganized confusion of thought would tend to keep your civilization at the level it is without countervailing forces. As energy increases, due to the prevailing cycle which is on an upward trend, then thought is forced to be clarified. Another way, of course, is to clarify thought and that is indeed the purpose of this book, so that the resulting strain is not necessary. Clear the thought, simplify the thought and one will "go with the flow." Have I confused you?

*"Not at all. If we all knew each other's thoughts, the nasty thinkers would soon be outcasts or change their thoughts."*

Each, then, in most cases, would be placed in a "time" corresponding to the development of his level of thought. For instance, at your level of thought today, it would be difficult for you to adapt and live one hundred years in the past or future. The only way one could ever adapt would be for the individual consciousness to master his ego and then universal intelligence would see to it that he could adapt to any time and place. You could call this type of being or spirit truly timeless.

Now, let us go into coding variables. How would you be identified by other beings?

*"By the way I look and the way I act."*

What if they ran into you or so they thought and they identified someone who looked just like you by the way they thought you should look? How far do you think the conversation would go before they decided it wasn't you?

*"Not far."*

For example, if I came to you and said I was Seth, how would you identify me?

*"By your voice and the particular type of energy I feel."*

If it were another energy, how far would it go, if it were the same voice, before you picked it up?

*"It would depend on how similar the energy's frequency was."*

So I would be, then, a series of coded variables called Seth. Is that correct?

*"Yes."*

Then John would be a series of coded variables or coded frequencies (thoughts) called John. Is this true?

*"Yes."*

Now, when I wish to speak to you, I would request to speak to the coded frequencies of Dotti. "Hi, coded frequency Dotti." I seek, of course, to robotize you. So, if your identical twin was viewed on the street by a friend, the only way that he would then recognize her is by her nonresponsiveness to his frequencies or codes. Does this make sense?

*"Yes. Seth, why did you bring this up?"*

Well, the reason is, once a thought is sent out, how would it know where to return? Isn't that a good question?

*"Yes, that is a good question. If I send out a thought that I want a new car, how will the car know where to find me?"*

So all beings are a coded system of thought. To find the sender of a thought, one would need know the code of the sender. Each thought has a series of codified variables which identify the "name and address" of the sender. These, of course, are attached to the access variable.

Now, one would have a genetic code, would they not? This identifies you as a Dotti, or a Dotti appearing individual. This code is part of the coded variable of the access code. Another part would be your individual frequency of vibration. The rest is your collective system of colored categories and nuance which identifies your individual focus. Now, do you need anything else in the way of identifying and categorizing thought? I know you don't know the answer, so I will supply it. It would need to find you in the right time. Now, what would happen if a thought were sent out in 1742 and didn't come back to you until 2016? This would clearly be a problem. Now, the universe has to take this into account as thoughts are timeless. Then some shading need go on to bring the thought according to need. Obviously, if someone did not put enough energy to a thought in 1742, a horse-drawn carriage might show up in 2016, as you indicated. This brings up a slight problem.

*"I want this car in this lifetime. I want to own it and I want it in this lifetime."*

Yes, that's right. Some sort of control variable need be placed on thought, so you might need timed thought in timelessness and then it is encoded properly so that your new car may not arrive 30,000 years later. This is kind of an interesting chain or train of thought to follow. If someone had access and could process thought at a high enough level and the material was not available in the physical world at that time, then a delay might be engendered. Let us say that someone invented a helicopter in 1300 or 1500 A.D., and the material to construct it was not available. It would still be invented, wouldn't it? What would happen then? The thought being powerful, would be timeless and at the time of need and probability, would then be manifested. You might say, then, that all is already invented or created and in time will manifest. Again, where do ideas come from?

*"Universal intelligence."*

This leads to another interesting idea. What comes first, the solution or the problem? What do you think, now?

*"The solution has to be there first; otherwise, you would not be able to create the problem."*

That is so powerful that it is worth a little explanation. All that is, is already there, but in time it has, of yet, not manifested. All that is, is in such a gigantic block that its very massiveness can only be peeled off and revealed a little at a time in linear fashion. That is to say, time is small and all is large and when all is revealed, time is no more.

Now, I didn't mean to digress to the subject of the linearity of time, but it only seemed appropriate to bring this in to show how coded time variables would facilitate the intersection of intelligence with universal knowledge.

On some plane, then, there are inventions that might be scheduled for a particular time. This is only in the realm of probable time, however. The etheric device that I mentioned, which you and others have used, was an example of something created that could not be brought into time because the material was not available to manifest it physically. So, one has the option to invent it etherically. Isn't that nice?

If you needed to see an image of Seth, I could create one that would fit your image and likeness of me. Now, I have no physical body, so I would code one that would fit into your etheric mind or vision that would fit your needs. I might have one that you would like me to be. I might have one that I would like you to see me be.

Is that clear?

*"Yes."*

So we are speaking of coded images, aren't we? These codes then stick in your sphere and would identify the sphere of Seth or any other entity.

# CHAPTER 4

## DISSECTING THOUGHT

It is incumbent upon beings when seeking to understand thought in its pure form to begin to learn how to reduce it to the smallest fraction of energy. Now, thought, as we have seen, is composed of many parts of energy. When a thought is formed, stored, released and completed, it has taken what would be a very long journey in time. As we have seen, thought is not always of time. Upon most occasions, it takes on a timeless vein. This is necessary for its speedy completion.

Now, let us pull a thought apart. Let us take the thought which is this ice bucket over here. What is the thought composed of? The thought would seem simple at first, for it is a picture of an ice bucket. It is brown, it is brass, it has a certain size and shape and it has a handle that moves. There are many different materials involved with the ice bucket. But a part of the thought and the ice bucket would take on a number of different forms. Now, it looks solid and stationary to your physical eyes, but in essence, it is but energy placed into form by its intertwining electrical attractions bringing in color, hue and a number of different bonding energies which hold it together in time.

Now, what do you think the shape of this ice bucket would be in two hundred of your years? Would you know?

*"Maybe a sleeker, improved version."*

Without the thought holding it together, it would soon dematerialize. Now, this is probably not a believable statement.

Some explanation is needed. How was it created originally? In the case of all of the parts, it was formed by various thought energy which resulted in physical effort. Now, you would say that everyone knows this. I would agree up to a point, but what would appear as a solid, physical object is really not if you could view it correctly. Now, I see it as a bunch of rapidly moving particles adhering to a particular time and space, bonding it together and keeping it formed physically for a time. What I am really saying is that I see it as manifested energy only.

How does this process work? Someone has a thought, "I need something that would hold ice for a time. I do not need a refrigerator, as it is too big and cumbersome. What I need is something that would hold ice and could be transported from place to place easily and would keep it cold for some period of time, maybe two hours." Someone's thought actually created something that would be like this ice bucket. This started the process in motion. Someone had need to fill a void of creativity. That is, an inventor had need to invent something. So far, we are speaking of beings. These beings had need to express. Now, energy capable of forming material such as plastic, brass, iron, also had a void or a need to express. So we have then found that energy has potential to express and would seek to express itself. As we intimated before, expression in effect is activation or accessing and all energy has this potential. The universe then becomes the sorting mechanism. Creativity being energy also seeking to express itself, has the theoretical potential to bring into manifestation every type of ice bucket but probably would restrict it to a few shapes and colors. Now, why would it be restricted? Do you know?

*"To avoid flooding the market."*

Yes, balance comes into play. Too many ice buckets might mean too few pictures or chairs. Creativity needs to express itself in balance. The creative need potential is generated and when its accessing is complete, then need is resolved and all forces come back into balance. Yes, the universe seeks all things to balance. Each thought then would be its own balancing act or creative potential. Within each thought, it is known just how much energy is required to complete it or balance it. This process is not restricted to time and space. Someone around the world might suddenly start making brown ice buckets. Now, how would some-one in India, for instance, know that a brown ice bucket could be sold in the United States? He might know of ice buckets and sud-denly start producing them. How would he know how many to produce and where to send them? As can be seen, it is clear from our ice bucket example that there are forces at work which are un-seen and would balance with other forces which are energy, until potential comes into fruition. This may sound like a wordy description of what would seem at first to be but a simple con-cept. The problem is, of course, how to keep all energy expressing and at the same time, in balance. Have you ever thought about this?

*"Yes."*

And you have mentioned that large stores, in effect, generate a certain number of items of particular shape and color that hopefully would exactly match demand. How would they know this? They would know it by experience and another factor that we will call intuition. If one's intuition were off and you had a large store, one store would soon become out of balance and would not exist any longer. All forces would then have had their potential fulfilled and there would no longer be any imbalance between supply and demand.

All things work the same in the universe. Let us take, now, a colony of ants. To keep the colony functioning, certain needs need to remain in balance. The supply of air, heat, humidity and food, all of which are energy, need to be in balance. A simple system of thought communication conveying need to the various members of the colony causes them to express their energy in a collective fashion that results in the survival of the colony. In the absence of any exterior force, the colony would remain in balance. If more workers are needed, they are produced. If more of the generating variety are needed, they are produced. The potential of each is in-herent in the sphere of influence of each member of the colony. If there is no further need for the function of a colony of ants, an "exterior" force would be an instrument in its removal. All things created have purpose and need and without them, would soon return to a form of pure energy. The ants are but an example, but many animals that you now regard as extinct, fall into this category as an interesting side light. Many animals formerly inhabiting the planet had a particular focus and time. When their purpose and need is no longer, then their energy is removed.

Need, as befits thought, fits into another category, probably not known to you. Let us try something.

(Seth conducts an experiment.)

Energy communicates. Energy has a need to fulfill itself, to interconnect with other energy. I conducted a two-fold experiment, didn't I?

*"Yes."*

The first one you know about, whereby at a distance of so many feet, you would experience a thought. The thought was fulfilling your need and mine. We interconnected our spheres of influence. Now, the other part of the experiment was conducted by John, some distance away. He interconnected with you at an unknown level to both of you and you transferred thought, each fulfilling the need of the other. Sometimes the interconnection can be so powerful as to mesmerize you or to make you sleepy for no apparent reason. This is the other timeless mode which would be a telepathic sphere of influence. If you have a need, it could be close by, such as a few feet or may be accessed with no time and space, depending on how that particular need would be energized. What if you had a need and you didn't know it? Do you think this need would be energized?

*"Yes."*

Yes. Now, someone suddenly would appear and he starts talking to you for no reason that is apparent. He talks long of a subject which you think is strange, say an odd disease and would explain all the ramifications of it in detail. You wonder during the conversation why he decided to talk of this subject. A few hours later, someone starts talking to you about the same subject, saying he doesn't know what to do about the problem concerning this subject. He wonders where to get this information and you are able to fulfill his need. A solution was handed to you verbally by the discussion with the first subject and you would be used as an instrument to fulfill the need of the second subject. You needed to help the second subject and the solution was presented prior to the stating of the problem by the second subject.

*"John had an experience with a dog that he had for a number of years and it finally died of old age. It was very difficult to let go of*

*the dog, as the dog had become so close to John that it had some human characteristics. One day, for no reason, when I was working with someone, I said, 'My husband had this old dog,' and relayed the whole experience. The woman I worked with then told me her experience with a very old dog that was still living. Right after that, another woman client showed up and I started talking about both experiences for no apparent reason. This was exactly what the woman needed to hear as she was having a traumatic experience letting go of an old dog with failing health that she knew would pass on."*

Now, this experience was conducted without benefit of time. You were used as an instrument to fulfill a need and the solution was presented to you prior to the need. This goes on all the time and we do not even think about it.

This type of experience is an example of the accessing form of telepathy in your timeless sphere of influence. Let us say you have a problem. In some cases, someone has already presented the solution to you. In all cases, the solution is already there, but you fail to see it. Think of that. Every problem of need is already solved. If one would know this, it would take away the need for time. Everything is in reverse from the way beings consciously think.

What are we saying here? We are saying that the energized particle already knows where to go, for instance to your sphere, prior to the conscious knowing that there is even a problem. Furthermore, that this is always the case and it is merely a matter of accessing the solution that is already there.

This is a bit confusing. To unravel this further, I need to relate a little example.

Here comes this energized particle that knows something. It is a solution in search of a problem. It goes looking for the probable path of the solution seeker. In the case of the dogs, it finds someone like you, with similar experience and seeks to fill you with the solution so that you can relay it in such a way that the seeker will know that the solution to the problem exists. Now, the solution particle then has been loaded with a lot of information or energy. It goes seeking along the probable path of the seeker, seeking to energize new intersections in a fashion that will again be attractive to the seeker.

Let us take your recent example with autism. The solution was given as a treatment for this disease. All of a sudden, one after the other beings enter or intersect your life seeking a solution to this disease. They suddenly start talking. It is to your surprise that all speak of the same subject. Did you wonder how this could happen?

*"It looks like the solution is connecting with the problem."*

That is correct, but it gets better. Because of fear, there is so much energy placed in avoiding the solution to problems that the problem gets greater and greater, robbing other areas of your lives of energy. Now, if one faced the fear of the solution, not only would it be the shortest path to the solution, it also would be the shortest path to your greatest growth. So much energy is placed in fear of finding the solution that little is left over for anything else. When the solution is faced, it creates a void that the universe then will rush in to fill with something surprising. This is growth in other areas that had a lack of energy because of the excess of energy that was placed in avoiding the solution. Facing the fear of this unmentioned problem we had discussed opens up so many other areas to your growth that you wouldn't believe me until you find out. So, what we have here is not fear of the problem, but fear of the solution, which is the very thing that beings profess to want. Beings fool themselves with this, deluding their thinking in a way that they would be solving the problem and in effect are avoiding the very thing they seek, out of fear.

Now, when healers heal the effect or the problem, then the cause or solution is neglected. *The fear of the solution* is so great at times that some beings will go from incarnation to incarnation avoiding solving the problem. What they do is roost in fear and fear is never into the solution. I am making the strongest point that I can possibly make in seeking the solution, no matter what it is, for the solution never has the negative effects of the fear of facing the problem. Never! If one would get this one point, all other things would melt away in significance, like wax from a candle. When the wax melts away, the light remains.

Now, as you know me, I am wont to mention something else. There may be, of course, more than one solution or probable solutions. A probable solution is the solution before it becomes fact. Then the solution becomes one where probable solution is fact.

The probable solution that becomes fact is the one that is the most attractive. By being most attractive, I mean the one that stands out when the fear is set aside. One can put facts down on paper and this has the tendency to disarm egotistical fear and then sometimes the solution is there. At other times, the solution is not apparent and one would stand back, after asking for help and the solution is presented in a way that you would probably never believe would transpire.

So, we have learned that solutions are energized probable particles that are engendered with divine intelligence in search of completion. Now, these states not only arrive in your conscious, walking around condition, but also enter your dream and/or vision conditions. Let us say that you wake up and you remember a certain part of your dream. At first appearance, it would seem to be a random collection of thought that entered with no clear message for you. Have you ever had dreams like this?

"*Yes.*"

So, dreams that you remember have a message for you to interpret that would lead you to face a particular problem that consciously you could not. Now, I don't wish to get into a long interpretation of dreams here. But the collection of thought arranged in a sequence by picture or feeling is important to let you see how you are living just below the surface. If you would write these down, placing every detail of them on paper, it won't be long before your internal guidance will help you understand what is not clear in your awake state. Little clues are presented, such as brightness, condition of buildings, old or new and what state of repair they are in. All scenes, be they in the dream state or awake state, are bringing in energy so that your internal receptors can process them in a way that would make them accessible to you.

Your phone rings and someone starts speaking about some problem that he or you might have. This may seem inconsequential, but the release of energy sets many energized particles in motion. The conversation engenders thought and ideas that may encompass a great many intersections and involve hundreds of beings, causing many thoughts to come into completion. This leads to an interesting subject. This subject, let us label probable expectations. This can cause many events to take place. Expectation is usually generated by fear. One starts expecting a particular result and this would be generated by thoughts that are not in concordance with each other. During the phone conversation, someone mentions, "Did you know what happened to Ellen?" And you would say, "No. What happened to Ellen?" He answers, "She has this disease and probably, she won't live much longer." Now, that thought goes out seeking Ellen and Ellen, on some level of consciousness, will pick it up. Now, Ellen, just having something minor, suddenly gets depressed and begins to fear that her minor ailment might be serious. The probable expectation put forth by the phone caller is not based on any fact and would have the tendency to make a situation that would be minor, to be of consequence. It wouldn't be long and all would be saying, "Poor Ellen." Of course, Ellen would not know any of this. It would seem that all had ganged up upon her and seek to enliven her disease. So, in effect, others would expect to live her life for her and under pseudo good wishes, seek to bring about her demise. Now, Ellen's body, sitting there with Ellen in it, would wonder why she is getting worse when subconsciously all she wanted was a brief rest from stress. Have you ever heard of a situation like this?

*"Yes, I have taken part in situations like this."*

Few know of the consequence of probable expectations. There are minor consequences such as traffic jams. But there are major ones, also, such as tragic calamities.

Now, let us take a traffic jam, considering probable expectations. If one would travel down a road at a given place, at a given time and see a traffic jam, one would engender a probable expectation of a traffic jam. So, if one comes to the same place at the same time the next day, one would expect a traffic jam. Now, if two beings encountered the same event or intersection on two successive days, then the traffic jam would be that much more probable because each would slow down at the decided place unexpectedly expecting the jam. Now, if there were no jam, they would be surprised but it still would be encased within their sphere and they would go on "probably expecting" the jam for some time, even though they are unaware of it. If one would continue to go on with three or more beings expecting a traffic jam, it would not be long before there would be a traffic jam for no apparent reason, at a fixed time every day.

Now, let us say these beings would travel this road five days per week and only occasionally on Saturdays. What do you think would happen on Saturday at the same time?

*"Nothing."*

Wrong. The same thing would happen because, and this is interesting, not only would beings have expectations, the time and place would have expectations and this is amazing. Think of the ramifications of this. Not only for this type of event, but in various places where there is no physical reason for a traffic jam.

Now, let's say a being put out a thought for a new car. Following what I mentioned previously, a particularly affirmative thought is released. Right afterward, the thought comes in, "Oh, this can't really happen!" Woe is the being, for he has disconnected the first thought. Thoughts put forth with no belief/faith behind them are inconsequential and are soon disconnected. Then you might ask, "Where is my new car? I put in the order for it. Why hasn't it arrived?" Sadly, this is what takes place on a common basis. Now, if you concentrated on it hard enough, you could actually create a traffic jam right out in front of your house. Wouldn't that be fun? Think of what else this applies to.

*"It could influence the weather and many events."*

Now then, if one saw an event occur, let us say a plane ride, time after time with no mishaps, expectation would probably result. Beings would start thinking that sooner or later, something would happen to this plane, on this plane. As each event passes, the probable expectation of a mishap increases and with the increasing emotional charge, a probable event comes to pass. This has happened recently, in time, whereby every effort was made to ensure the successful completion of a flight, but tragedy occurred because of the probable expectation of a mishap building to a cresendo of emotional charge bringing the mishap into fruition.

Now, the universe has no judgment concerning such events. It merely seeks to complete the energy generated, whether it be what you would regard as on a positive or a negative scale.

Now, let us see this influence called expectation working on one to the other. Let us say that on a given day, you feel very good about yourself. You go out into the world with a smile on your face and happiness in your heart. The first being you encounter has a sullen look upon his face and utters a series of grunts which is about the best he can do on this given day. Your light mood slips a little but you are willing to "white" him out, so as to speak. Then along comes being "B" and he also utters a series of barely audible grunts and has a sullen expression. Your mood slips a little more and a little tiredness might start to creep in. If you continued with two or three more sullen beings like this, before long you might look just like them. The energy exuded by beings in this mood or hue would be heavy and of a variety that would influence the color of your sphere, hence a darker mood. If you could view this as I do, your spheres would be as a kaleidoscope with many different colors or hues. It would be but a simple matter if you were I, and I will teach you this eventually, you could inject a lighter, brighter color into your sphere and brighten yourself right back up. If you knew the frequency you were in at a given time and you knew the frequency that would correspond to your lighter, brighter moods, you could do it with music. Music is a series of colorations or hues based on frequency which will intersect at a given level of your sphere. If you knew of a particular piece of music that if you played it consistently, it would brighten your mood, you would then know that this music had the proper frequency to brighten you up. There are those who know this information and could brighten you up without much effort. One could also use color, incorporating tones, if one had the right information.

Now, beings have much difficulty with uncontrolled moods. Let us do an experiment.

(Seth picked up the divining rods and pointed them over my head. I felt energy more on one side than the other. Then Seth adjusted the energy over my head until it was about equal. I felt my head elevate and my mood brightened.)

What I did here was project some gold energy over your head, overloading your sphere with it, which would automatically enable you to lift yourself up. When one elevates his consciousness in this way, one automatically would brighten his mood. You are going to ask me a question, aren't you?

*"Sure. I'd like to be able to do this whenever I feel the need."*

All right then. Have John pick up the divining rods and point them over your head and project gold by thinking it or by looking at a golden sheet or any gold object. This has the reverse effect of those you would run into in a dark mood who would bring you down.

As we have already discovered, places have energy. They might have a fixed energy as in traffic patterns or they might have lighter, brighter energy or dark energy. All things are influenced by colors or light as the case may be. If one goes to a nice beach, one generally would feel better. Do you know why?

*"Because you get gold energy from the sun and the sand."*

Brilliant. Now, I could mean you or the light. The beach is the place that has a natural cleansing effect upon the air so any negativity or negative energy would soon be washed away. This, coupled with reflection of the golden sun rays upon the water, the ultraviolet light in some cases, the colors, bring one into a happier, more energetic state of mind. Too much gold energy, unless you are used to it, could leave one feeling mesmerized.

Now, back to sound. If one had an instrument, one could play every note of an octave. Some note in this octave would be more to one's liking than any other. That would result in your frequency. It might be a sharp or a flat, but nevertheless, that is the closest thing to your frequency. Do you have a favorite color?

*"Light blue."*

All right then. If you would look at that color and play your favorite note, then it would bring about a feeling of well-being. That would be then the frequency at which you are most comfortable and most happy. Now, this could change from time to time, depending on your growth. Do not attach judgment to this. Any color and tone will do.

(Seth conducts an experiment.)

*He sat down at the piano after handing me a light blue pillow that we accidently happen to own. After going through the whole octave a few times, we hit upon the key of F. After hitting the note a few times, he then played a melody in the key of F while I stared at the blue pillow. This felt very pleasant.*

Well, indeed it should, for in effect, you heard and saw your vibration right at the moment. Once again, I need to reiterate just how powerful thought is. How would frequency be established unless one used level of thought?

Let us see how thought influences beings. Let us take a movie, for instance. If it were silent, then it would have merely the effect of energy and motion. Certain energy would be released, causing a mood or hue in you. If sound and color were added, they would add much depth of feeling. You would notice that as the scenes unfold, music is added, increasing the emotional charge or tension in an exciting scene such as a chase scene or it could be smooth and mellow along with a scene depicting a sunset. A romantic scene would have melodious music to accompany it. Do you know what I mean?

"*Yes.*"

The great musicians would know this and would seek to capture and enrapture you with scenes flowing through their music. Do you know what I mean?

(Seth conducts an experiment. During this experiment, two distinct pieces of music were played. The first one reminded me of a scene in the forest with white light shining in through tall trees. It was a very misty scene. The second piece of music brought to mind people involved in a celebration, heralding a new ruler in medieval times.)

So, now you see what I mean. Music has color and impresses thought and in effect, can help you picture events and/or moods. Who would have thought such a thing? Kidding, of course. If one were so inclined, one could compile a myriad of information using sound and color and one might indeed be surprised at the profound effects it would have on others.

Someone, somewhere along the line told you that you had trouble with your eyes after a certain age and you believed them. Did you know that?

"*I know it now.*"

So the preponderance of thought suggested to you that at a certain age that you might need reading glasses.

"*So, at that age, I got them.*"

It is quite remarkable, again with expectations, what will happen. One could devote a whole chapter to reversing expectations.

Your relationship to your fellow beings is governed by the thoughts you are thinking of yourself. If you are thinking well of yourself, even it you think you don't look good, the overwhelming preponderance of energy automatically convinces others of your well being and theirs. When you say you don't like someone, what is it that you don't like?

*"I don't like certain behavior."*

Their behavior is interconnected to you in a way. One would treat you one way and the same one would treat another another way. That is to say, the influence of your thoughts unspoken, the mood or hue, would somewhat influence their behavior. They would have certain feelings about you and their behavior would be governed accordingly. The master would be so in control as to influence all equally. By control, I mean the master would relieve control to be in control. He would allow the universe to be in control. It is one of my many purposes in bringing this information to you to show you the way to this state.

Now, when meeting others, rest assured then that they have something for you. This is not in the egotistical sense, but means that certain unconscious energy would be resting there ready to be imparted to others. This is the out of control area of beings. Have you seen that many beings would be or seem to be different from time to time?

*"Yes."*

Do you have any idea of why they would be different from time to time?

*"No."*

I will explain. First of all, where do you meet beings, your house, their house or a common meeting ground? You would meet then at a common meeting ground such as a place you both know and they would be different, wouldn't they? If you meet them in your house, they are different again. If you meet them at their house, they are different again. This would seem to indicate that there are all kinds of hidden influences brought to bear at any meeting. Now, we have already established in our hypothetical traffic situation that places are imbued with energy. If there is residue in the way of smoke or fumes left-over after cooking, would there not be energy residue left-over from your presence or others? Your house has certain frequencies of energy. It intersects or influences what takes place here. For instance, a certain conversation with another would have been influenced or colored by the energy already in residence here. There were those, and a few know this, who could impregnate the frequency of a place with a certain type of energy. This would be with conscious knowledge. But of course, so far your house is impregnated with energy of which you have little knowledge. This is so interesting. How long do you think that energy would remain at a particular place?

*"I haven't any idea."*

Good. For what happens is energy would act in a timeless fashion waiting for it to complete itself. This could take any amount of time, for the energy, be it thought or not, does not know the concept of time. Isn't that truly unbelievable? Energy in time, as you would regard it, really isn't in time. In effect, time is only a limited part of your function and you would be consciously aware of it. You walk in a certain place and you have a certain feeling. It would have influence upon you and you would have varying degrees of compatibility or non-compatibility. Why would you choose a particular house in a particular location?

*"Because the energy is attractive."*

Now, I have set you up for this somewhat, not to steal from your intelligence, but in truth, a house you might select could be non-appealing to most beings, but because of a particular type of energy that intersects pleasantly with yours, you would like it. You and John seem to like the same things, the same type of house and certain places to visit. You might say that this is most convenient that he likes the same things that you do. What it is, is both are of like energy and would necessarily like similar things. What I really should say here is similar intersections or influences.

Now, let us say that you are both interested in going to an old fort. One comes to mind, not too far from where you live. At this fort, there are in residence certain thoughts and energy which can be read. Now, you might say, "You are clearly off the track this time, Seth, for I read nothing." But, this isn't true, you see, for a few days later, certain information comes out of you that if anyone would have asked you, you would have no idea where it came from. Do you know the fort I have in mind?

*"Fort Point in San Francisco."*

Now, in residence there were certain stories and energy depicting life at a certain time there. Did you get any feeling from the place?

*"John filled in several feelings of the place."*

All can accomplish the same thing, picking up energy from various places. You do this already, but you don't realize you are. By picking up this energy, you can decipher it by standing back, taking a deep breath and observing the feeling or seeing what story it has to tell you. Your house has a particular story in that many different sets of beings have lived here, taking into consideration its age. What is the feeling that you get about your house?

*"A very happy, open feeling."*

It is a place of healing, learning and growing. That is its particular energy.

Now, certain places on the planet have very strong energy points as many beings know. The great pyramid being one of these places, coincides with a vortex of energy that has great purpose.

Now, the energy of a place can also be captured by pictures, be they photographs or paintings. Where does that picture remind you of?

(Seth points to a picture on the wall.)

*"Cimarron Canyon in New Mexico."*

Even though the picture was captured in the mind or sphere of the painter, the energy interconnected with you in a way to generate a thought from your sphere.

As we have seen, places have energy on their own. Your family has a certain type of energy, also. They influence each other in a way that suggests that a particular frequency or frequencies are brought together for common interests. Your family influences each member, also, with its cohesive frequencies in more than just the waking state. You have noticed that when a member has a dream, other members of the family sometimes pick it up. They may fill in the missing pieces. You might say that families influence each other with colors and certain moods.

When the family was reassembled, you noticed certain new influences for the common good. Children now think differently than before and their previous programmed thinking is being reprogrammed along new lines. Yes, they have been together before in another incarnation or more. I am sure this doesn't surprise you at this juncture, for that is what I meant by being reassembled.

Each group of beings that would surround your family would bring certain thought energy to bear on each member and it is processed by your various spheres in a way that generates additional growth.

Now, you were guided to another location recently which would generate new influence in the most efficient, rapid manner for your joint growth. Certain lessons were learned in this locale to do with structure, schedule and discipline which then furthered all of your joint greater being. If one were to align himself intuitively with the energy that would guide one and flow with it, forgetting about any probable outcome, it would be surprising at how easily things then flow and the pieces fall into place just like it would be directed by the leader of a great orchestra. If one lets go and watches the flow of seemingly disconnected events, the unexpected outcome would be conducive to much happiness.

There is an intelligence in the universe that would dissect and direct your every thought. By putting space between thoughts, one then connects one's self to the flow of the mystical light. What do I mean by this? Do you know?

*"I'm learning it."*

What do you think I meant by mystical light?

*"Do you mean guiding light?"*

Yes, I do mean guiding light. Do you know how to connect with it?

*"No."*

Within each, there is a particular frequency that you need get in touch with that shows you the solution to a particular problem. Sometimes, the problem hasn't arrived yet, but you can expect that when you might see this, it will. Take your favorite color, for instance, and see if you can get a material object that closely represents this. Think of a problem and then focus on the light, letting go of the problem and the solution will manifest itself in the particular frequency of which you asked. This frequency coincides with your favorite color if you have become familiar with it. This will let you know when you are on the right track. Now, how does this work?

The solution aligns itself with a particular frequency that is designated by you. Most are unaware of this. The frequency may have the hue of a feeling or you may just see the color. Directing thought energy to align itself with your favorite frequency has the effect of laying a track on which the solution is rolled out. This takes some conscious training of your mind. If one would focus on his favorite color and let go, then the response would be dictated in the range of that particular color frequency. The only interference to this process would be colorations imposed by your ego, such as emotion of some kind. Anger comes to mind. Sometimes, depending upon the evolution of each being, there would be a delay in time. Rest assured, however, that this process cannot help but to work, for it directs thought along a certain frequency aligning it for a specific purpose. This, in effect, is always powerful.

Some have honed their thinking to a degree that they have a certain "feeling" about something. That certain feeling can hold one in good purpose and the practice with it hones their skill to the degree that they begin to have faith in it, recognizing probable results.

Let us say one is driving down the road and unbeknownst to him, there is an obstacle ahead causing a traffic jam a few miles up the road. Just prior to leaving, one encountered an unexpected delay which irritated him, for it would seem to take a lot of time to resolve. Maybe the toilet suddenly overflowed and you need to spend energy to fix it. You could have two choices here: Let it go and rush out the door or you could leisurely look over the situation, allowing your greater self to come into play accessing certain solutions. The calmness of your attitude would tell you which of the alternatives would be the best way. If you felt anxious about being delayed and attempted to go anyway, you would suddenly find yourself in this traffic jam. If you did the opposite and coolly assessed the situation with the toilet, then the resulting delay would cause you to miss the traffic jam that the universe was attempting to make known to you. How many times have you rushed somewhere only to find yourself delayed and you became increasingly frustrated at being so "late?" Without putting forth energy to intentionally make yourself late, you will usually find that the universe has arranged that the delay is beneficial for all involved. Do you know how this works?

*"No, I haven't been able to figure this out."*

The universe in its unlimited, intelligent way, knows of your destination and the destination of any being or place where you are to intersect for your common good. Now, this is saying a lot, for it is saying that every thought is in touch with every other thought and that is how it works, exactly. On some level, when you think of a place, you intersect the energy of the place. When you think of a person, you intersect the energy of that being. On some level, then, you both, energy and being, decide on the most beneficial outcome for both of you. Now, do not take this to mean that you do not have choice, for the ego enters to gum up the works. Without the false self, all would function perfectly, but the false self would seek to dismember it by assuming control when it does not have the greater intelligence necessary to assume control. It cannot even control its small self. It is not even aware of universal intelligence. It fools itself into falsely thinking that it has anything to do with achieving any solution or end result. The unfortunate thing for beings is, it has constructed a massive mechanism of deception which would fool itself into thinking it can provide the outcome of its false choices.

Now, we have been discussing dissecting thought. What we have not discussed is false thought. False thought would be thought that was generated without sufficient intelligence to complete itself. It is the mission of every being to attempt to not use false thought. We are differentiating here between thought with purpose and thought without purpose. Egotistical, idle thought would generate energy to a degree but comes from such a level that it leaves the request without power and without much meaning. It is a safeguard placed within the sphere of most incarnated beings that thought of this nature would not be of sufficient charge to bring about destructive energy. It would take much thought by many beings to influence a probable outcome where cohesion would exist to provide a calamity. Love, being the most powerful force in the universe, necessarily comes from the higher, lighter frequency and hence its completion has a much higher probability.

When beings put their energy into attempting to decipher their conscious thoughts in a directed, simple manner, the probable outcome for such efforts with purpose will result in the generation of higher frequency of thought energy. Again, the higher the frequency of thought from which we live, the happier beings live and the easier, efficient flow of energy is manifested.

# CHAPTER 5

## WHY THOUGHT IS IMPORTANT

The importance of thought is nearly always underestimated by beings. And why is this?

*"Because we don't realize how powerful these thoughts are."*

Since you already know the subject, you suspected the question was loaded, didn't you?

*"I was busy trying to think of the right answer. But I think that, as we go through the day, we forget that our thoughts have power. If I make a mistake, I automatically think, 'Oh, I am so stupid,' not realizing what that thought does to me. I forget."*

When you would have this thought, "I am so stupid," where do you think it goes?

*"I don't even think about it, but if I did, I would say that having that thought could literally make me stupid because I think it. And it could influence anyone around me to think I was stupid, even if I didn't say it out loud."*

Yes. Now, thought which was unguarded drifts upward and inward. Let us examine what can happen. Buried now within you is some energy that is coded, "I am stupid." Projected outward is the same thought form. In your surrounding sphere of influence is added this energy. As you walk down the street, you project this on two levels.

Let us say that during the same day, you accomplish something of brilliance. Then the thought, "I am brilliant," enters the same two spheres, doesn't it?

*"Yes."*

So then, as you are taking the walk down the street, you have two messages in your aura or sphere, don't you?

*"Yes."*

So, now in your sphere is the dual message, "I am stupid; I am brilliant." If these were the only two entrenched thought forms in and around you and you ran into another being, causing what I call an intersection, what would they think?

*"They would be confused."*

Do you see why there would be some confusion on this planet with thought?

*"I sure do."*

(Seth gets up and walks across the room as a Simulated Being. Here comes the Simulated Being.)

"Hi, I am John. I am a stupid and I am a brilliant being."

*"What!"*

Now, in a simple way, do you realize that is what actually happens?

*"I never realized this so clearly before. I thought I could hide my negative thoughts from others by saying positive things."*

Yes. Now, the person observing this half-stupid, half-brilliant being, would remark after passing, "Gee, there goes a half-stupid, half-brilliant being. How do I deal with that, being a half-stupid, half-brilliant being myself? Do I deal with the brilliant side or the stupid side?"

Now, we have only discussed two thoughts. In actuality, how many do you think beings would have on a given day?

*"Thousands."*

Yes. What do you think the being that you meet, knowing this, would actually think then?

*"I think the being would feel uneasy about me and himself, unless he was very secure."*

Yes. What he would probably think is, "Here comes a myriad pile of thought. I don't think I can deal with this."

Now, complicating this is the emotional charge put on these various thoughts. It is like shooting them with a quiver of arrows, indiscriminately. "George, you really are a rotten person." George hears, "I am brilliant," and George says, "Thank you very much." Then you say, "When did you go off the track?"

George replies, "You're right, it is a beautiful day." Clear as mud. Do you think this actually happens?

*"It happens to me many times a day. I'm constantly talking to people who tell me one thing verbally, but I pick up the opposite feeling from them and know they're not telling the truth. But until now, I didn't realize that they are catching me, too."*

What is not known is that this energy is put into the stockpile surrounding this planet, from which all beings draw. What effect do you think this would have?

*"I can't really think in terms of the effect that everyone's misthoughts would have on this planet. I'm too busy with my daily struggle, trying to figure out where I'm at and what the people I run into are trying to say."*

(Communication stops as Seth practically inhales a muffin.)

The planet has a stockpile of energy and within that stockpile are all thoughts that ever were and ever shall be. Can you imagine waking up in the morning and being hit by a few of these?

*"I've had mornings like that."*

So buried within and without are disparate thoughts that sometimes crop up at the most inopportune times and from places unknown. Do you see why this country has a need for psychiatrists?

*"Yes. Unfortunately, the same myriad pile of thoughts is probably hitting the psychiatrists, too."*

Now, let us say that ten years ago, you made an error in your checkbook that cost you nine hundred and some dollars. And you said, "I am so stupid," with a real charge behind it. The greater the emotional charge behind the thought, the deeper is its impregnation in the subconscious, making it more difficult to uproot.

(Starting again, two days later, Seth appears very bright, cheerful and full of energy, so to speak.)

Now, as the thought, which was charged heavily by the emotions, entered the storage place of the subconscious, imagine it as a drill penetrating the surface of the planet in search of oil. The stored energy is on many levels. With our analogy, it (pause) goes without saying that the deeper one probes, the more difficult it is to reach the stored energy.

Imagine, now, a major shock in your life. Let us say, the death of your mother. The event leaves such a mark that it may be overlooked at the time as being significant. Years later, out comes the thought, "I really miss my mother." Now, where does this come from?

*"I don't know, but I'd like to know because I have had this experience."*

Oh, I know.

(Seth is now rolling around the kitchen floor in his chair, which has wheels on it. Good thing I have kids and am used to this. Otherwise, it could throw me off.)

This deeply buried thought from out of nowhere, seemingly, was stored there by a mechanism that only the mind knows. Each thought is placed there with a code that is triggered in a way that no one understands. It is a form of association, but unless one has the code, it (the thought) would be unreachable. It would be in a kind of cave with an entrance to be gained only by this code. Now, how do you think one could reach these thoughts?

*"Learn the code."*

Yes.

(Seth again scoots across the floor in the chair. He's obviously happy, so I must have given the right answer.)

How do you learn the code?

*"Ask you for it."*

Indeed.

*"Seriously, I would like to know the code. I've had problems all my life due to what I think of as repression of feelings."*

All right. When I say the word "slam" and gesture, this then brings the ego to the now moment. Then I will pick any word. Let us use the word "nuance," and a word then comes to mind from you. What would that be?

*"Avoiding."*

Yes. Now, this word then triggers another and this sets the coding mechanism into gear. I then pick another word "fear" and you would say . .

*"Losing."*

Yes. Now, I do not wish to go beyond this for now because I will then lose you to the coding process. But let us describe how this works.

(Seth gets up and lets the dog in.)

I can pick any word and you will then tell me the code counterpart. When I mention another word, it could be any word which is common, then you have another one automatically to follow.

If you define the problem area for which you wish to discover the solution, then pick a few words with this in mind. It will become clear when you reach the problem area, which words are the keys. If you reach a problem area of anger, then the word red becomes a key. If you reach a problem area where the word jealousy is a problem, then the words envy or green are the keys. To clarify, with most deep problems, it will take five or six word associations to reach the level. Then you use the same words associated with the problem, another five or six, over and over, until the solution presents itself. It may be necessary to repeat this process a number of times until the solution is manifest. The solution is readily apparent because it will provide a strong release of energy. Is this not true?

*"Yes. I knew when I found it."*

There are sometimes pictures of places or feelings of events that are presented along the trail. The deeper problems are covered over with many layers, cleverly placed there by the conscious mind, which was overwhelmed at not being able to solve the problem. The problems are buried, you see, as if in a graveyard. The conscious mind believes out of sight, out of mind. In reality, the problem is only buried to begin growing greater tendrils which reach out and bother the conscious mind periodically.

Now, again, if the problem were buried with enough emotional charge, it then becomes a driving force in the life of the one who has buried it. Unless beings are at one with themselves, they are driven by the subconscious thoughts.

There are beings with enough of these emotionally charged thoughts buried within their subconscious which we would brand as crazy. The ego would put off the solution of these problems to the point that it would overwhelm the subconscious and something would have to break. Fortunately, in most cases, the soul steps in and renders the solution to the conscious mind which then congratulates itself as brilliant. The conscious mind does not even know whence it came.

It is obvious that the storehouse of the subconscious mind is vast, indeed. Material is taken from this storehouse and placed in dreams, in visions and is mixed and matched with one's daily experiences. In addition, thought from other incarnations is sometimes intermixed or flows through, resulting in confusion or the release of new knowledge. The very vastness of this storehouse makes it possible to store millions of energetic particles known as thought. The mix and match process goes on through a series of codes, something like a computer, that becomes more obvious with the use of our decoding process. All of this is virtually automatic, you see. There are many levels of this, not all are easily accessible. On some level is coded every thought or experience. It is only a matter of learning to push the right buttons and it will be released to the limited conscious mind which is only capable of a few thoughts at a time. When a thought comes in, it comes in the form of energy that is then coded and dispensed to the proper area as would befit its emotional charge. There is kind of a sorting area where the energy is then matched with other stored energy and the process then accumulates the energy in the right storage bank.

Now, with some beings, there would almost be grooves worn to channel in a certain kind of energy. Let us say that the anger storage unit is much more filled than others. When an angry thought comes in, there is a more direct link to the storage area than with another type of thought. A magnetic charge would be strewn through to the surface which would clearly attract other similar charges. Once this process gets into operation, then this particular being would be deemed an angry person and would attract angry thought. It is, by this time, almost a self-generating procedure where anger begets anger.

Now, at some point, the circuit would become overcharged and short out. What do you think would happen then?

*"The person would explode with anger or catch a disease."*

Yes. When the circuit shorts out, then it will be one or the other. The energy has to be released, one way or the other. Violence erupts or disease occurs.

Other forms of fear may be brought in in this fashion. The common thread is an emotional charge. A shock buried the thought ever so deeply and then other thoughts are channeled into the groove until this area becomes unbalanced or overloaded. Then a release mechanism discharges the overload, causing the reaction.

Now, you can see how every being professes certain characteristics. How do you like that?

*"I like it."*

Now, wouldn't you know that it isn't only what you might call negative thought that would work in this way. Happy thought is attracted in the some way. Let us try this.

(Seth conducts an experiment.)

Now, let us try the word "fulfillment."

*"Okay."*

"Regarding."

*"Happiness."*

"Complete."

*"Peace."*

Now, let us see how this ties in. What is underlying? "Arrange."

*"Situations."*

Now, what have we done here? Do you find the peace flowing in and through you?

*"I'm thinking that the peace depends on righting certain situations."*

I think the same thing. Isn't that remarkable?

(Seth draws on my cigarette. The doorbell rings and Seth answers it. The mailman doesn't realize who he is talking to!)

Now, as we were speaking, did, in fact, it work?

*"It pointed out that there is something in the way of my feeling peaceful today."*

That is exactly right. So, did that work?

*"Yes."*

Okay. Now, I have proven my point, have I not?

*"Yes."*

Now, here is the crux of the matter. It matters not what takes place external to thought, for it does not, you see. The deeply entrenched thought is from which you live. Do you understand this?

*"I understand it, but I'm not always able to do it."*

Oh. Now, as I've led you out of that, what has changed?

*"I don't know."*

Now, you thought you were thinking of one thing, didn't you?

*"Yes."*

But you were thinking of something else. Almost all beings

have this difficulty. Shall we get to what you were really seeing?

"*Yes.*"

You will find this fascinating. All right, here it comes. "Johnny-mail."

(Seth conducts another experiment.)

Now, we have conducted an experiment. By word association, we have gone through to the level where the now moment was tied into a moment from your past. What was the connecting link? Guilt, wasn't it? Now, you carefully entrusted me with your pile of guilt. I lifted it up to where the sun illuminated it and carefully placed it in another room. When I did this, the situation looked different to you, did it not?

"*Yes.*"

Look at how important that particular group of thoughts was in controlling how you felt today. Did I not prove that thought actually was controlling you?

"*Yes.*"

Good.

Now, each being has his own private reservoir of stored thought. Within each reservoir are happy and sad charged thoughts. When one or the other is triggered, they automatically are strung together in a fashion that might show one that he is controlled much as a robot would be controlled. Each day is a series of robotically controlled thoughts and motions, triggered by extraneous thoughts and events. Thought is out of control. Life is out of control along with it.

Did you know this was the way you were ruled?

"*No.*"

Now, if each being is controlled in this fashion, it would seem that even more destruction or uncontrolled emotions might be running rampant on this planet. What do you think keeps this in check?

"*I don't know.*"

I know. Counterbalancing this is something of "stuff" that comes through the soul, a balancing energy that carries the thrust of uncontrolled thought in a manner that creates some stability. As the thoughts are chained together forming a particular controlling pattern for a particular being, the soul of this being produces a counterbalancing thought which tends to neutralize the direction of the chained thought. Now, what would the soul attempt to construct? Have you any idea?

*"No."*

I thought not. The soul would allow those thoughts that would be most beneficial for the growth of the incarnation pattern, to learn.

Now, what would and who would actually be in control now?

*"I don't know."*

That is a good answer. For sometimes the soul would direct, but many times, the ego would win out. Overall, in most cases and eventually in all cases, the soul takes control.

With but a few examples, I have shown you that not only is thought important, it just is about everything. Thought controls, it is stored, it neutralizes, it becomes, it regresses and it is the transducer of information from within and without.

# CHAPTER 6

## GROUPING OF THOUGHT

Now, as has been discussed, it is easy to see that the grouping of thought along certain lines is aligned by beings according to certain characteristics that are reflected in the personality of the being in question. Now, what thought groups have been strongest within you?

*"Control."*

I like control, especially since this is an area whereby beings believe that they "control" their own destiny. Now, as we have discussed some of the aspects of thought patterns, it comes to mind that there are a variety of thoughts over which you have no control at all. How much in control of your life do you think you are?

*"I have no control at all. Of that I am convinced."*

Are you absolutely convinced that you have no control at all?

*"Yes."*

Now, obviously you have been set up, haven't you? What the ego says and what greater you would say are two different things. What governs the way you dress, the way you type, the way you eat and your relationship with John?

*"Well, I have some control. I have choice in those matters."*

Where does your choice come from?

*"I don't know."*

Would it come from an area that controls you and you not control it? Would it come from certain patterns that are grouped within you that would delineate your every action? Indeed, it would. I must have some control within me, also, for it would seem in the parlance of spirit to use the word "indeed." Now, there is a group of thought within you that would control you and you not control it. There is an intertwining or chain of thought linked in a manner that would subtly or grossly control your behavior. Some of this thought is yours; other thoughts are put there externally. By externally, I say those that you have taken in from the physical world. The controlling group of thought is the most important group for beings to take control of. Let us experiment. If I say "control," what would your response be?

*"Fear."*

"External."

*"False."*

"Internal."

*"Determining."*

You didn't know where the words would lead, but here is how it works. You clearly knew that external control was false. But internal control caused some hesitancy, as it would in most beings. When the word "determining" came out, it merely pointed out that it was in the works who was to take control, greater you or lesser you. Isn't that interesting? This would seem to indicate that you are in the process of change.

Within each being, then, is this control group that would interweave through every aspect of your life. Sometimes anger would take control and color the mechanism. Sometimes love would take control and color the mechanism accordingly. You could go through every emotion and you could see that this would then determine the control of the group. Throughout your culture, the terms "take control" or "control yourself" are important words. But up to this point, they are merely words, aren't they? I'll illustrate.

"Control yourself." What does it mean to you?

*"You're out of line. Get with it."*

How about the words "take control?"

*"I would take that as friendly advice."*

So many beings have but little understanding of the meaning of these terms. Now, if you wished to take control of a depressing mood, you would attempt to color it in a different fashion from the existing mood. You, of course, could do this by using tone and color as we suggested earlier. Another way would be to attack the fear surrounding the solution. Another perhaps more provocative method would be to start with the word most closely if not exactly representing the mood and working downward through the sphere using other words associated with color until one struck the right chord and it would elicit a strong emotional charge.

The control group of thought is interlaced entirely throughout your sphere, placed in strategic locations that would release or block your thought. The control group would then access or not access certain thoughts. So in effect, depending on the word or charge associated with the control thought would leave a door closed or open. There might be two words to release a particular blocked thought, kind of like having two keys to open a door. If some unfortunate being ever happened to utter two words that would unlock one of these time bombs within any other being, God help him. The mind or sphere places these thoughts of great charge within what it would regard as a secure area requiring an unusual combination to open it. There is much effort or thought placed in the thought to control the unleashing of this emotional charge. Some of the locked charges have the potential of releasing such great energy that if suddenly unlocked, they might cause what you would call a nervous breakdown. As you can see, the mind or sphere has an elaborate control mechanism. There are easily far more accessible controlling thoughts than any other.

There have been instances where it would be easy to see how the sphere is colored. There are beings who with a sample of a particular type of red would be induced almost to a state of frenzy with anxiety. The red is, of course, associated with a very dramatic event, perhaps with the letting of blood. By your expression, it appears that I have said something gross. Is that right?

*"Not really. I was actually worried about a typographical error I just made."*

Oh, I forgot the way you think. Now, beings could influence their capacity to vibrate higher into brighter thoughts by staring at gold objects or infusing themselves with gold light. Gold has a powerful effect when bathed upon the sphere. In most cases, unless the controlling group of thought is entrenched in the lower modes of color, gold will have a potent, beneficial effect toward raising to lightness or higher thought. Have you ever tried this?

*"Yes, and it worked."*

Let there be no misunderstanding that I would refer to the monetary aspect of gold color, for brass would do nearly as well. When one would be in the anger state, a switch to violet may induce him to become more spiritual. "Hi, Joe. How are you feeling today?" "I am fine, Dotti, I am feeling very violet." This would seem very strange, but would probably be closer to truth than, "Hi, I am a very stupid, very brilliant being. How are you?" Wouldn't you agree?

*"I am laughing so much that I don't know whether I agree or disagree."*

Color is quite important in control of thought. As has been shown by some beings, the color pink would serve to control violent behavior for a time. Obviously, this color would put beings in the love mode and would restrain them by this display.

Now, what if you could throw color at beings and influence their thoughts? "Hi, Joe. Have a smack of yellow." "I am fine, Dotti. Have some green." "I didn't offer you any money, but why is that sun so bright?" Another inane conversation by Seth. What does this mean? It means we actually speak in colors. Did you know that?

*"No. So if someone appears to be shallow, they have a very limited color chart."*

Now you are getting it. They might be limited to red through green. Then we could say, "Here comes Mr. Red-Green." And then we could say, "There goes Red-Blue." Now, if one were so attuned, in effect, he could read this with the colors of one vibration. He would already know to whom he was speaking. Would you like to try an experiment?

(Seth picks up a light blue pillow, a pink sheet and several other colored objects.)

You associate the light blue with John and yourself. The pink stands for love. By flashing the two colors alternately, I can send love by color from John. Does that make sense? All right then. What would happen if I spoke the same words, but used different colors?

(Seth does this and it just doesn't work.)

What do you think has happened here?

*"You've shown me that people speak in colors."*

I've also shown you that beings speak one way, but color their thought in another, causing much confusion. All right, I'm going to try something. I'm going to speak to you in a particular color. In other words, everything I'm going to say to you is colored in this particular color. What color do you think I speak?

*"Pink."*

You're laughing. It worked, didn't it? So it just goes to prove you should think pink while speaking black. How do you think actors and actresses control their performance?

*"By coloring their behavior."*

With the direction of the soul, beings decide the lessons to be learned in a particular incarnation. If a particular soul decides that anger is to be overcome in a particular incarnation, it will arrange an event or events that will allow the buildup of an emotionally charged group of thought that you would know as anger. This might be a particularly large block that would become a controlling force in this being's life. As has already been mentioned, the controlling group of thought would be attuned to the anger group and the two would work in concert. Now, many beings would think this would be disconcerting. At the slightest provocation, such as dropping a yellow pencil, this being may become quite angry. Events such as going to the store, driving down the road or hearing a ringing telephone can set him off into an emotional frenzy. This could become such a controlling part of the sphere that it would nearly be second nature to our being. Those around him would think, "What an angry person." Naturally, the being in question would not see or be aware of any of this until something would trigger the emotional charge buried within him or he would receive enough feedback to know that there is a problem. The other case would be some form of disease striking at the excess stress. The most difficult problem with these groups is that it is deceiving to beings believing that each event would strike a new chord instead of realizing that it strikes the same one. All of these chords are tied together. It sometimes takes such major trauma to reach the awareness of the subject that it may take more than one incarnation to learn the lesson. What does one do once he is aware there is a problem?

*"What do they do or what should they do? They usually repress the feeling because they're afraid to face the solution."*

That is correct. When one starts burying all of these emotionally charged thoughts, the charge builds up as I have mentioned, until a veritable explosion could result.

Now, once awareness strikes, one is free to start exploring the solution. One could start poking around, attempting to understand what is behind the particular behavior. The unfortunate thing is that so little is known about spheres that it has taken a painstaking process, sometimes years, before the buried cause pops out. Now, in subjects I have worked with, it is but a simple matter to associate words until the key pops out.

When we tried this with you, what happened?

*"What happened depended on the amount of emotional charge I had attached to the problem."*

Now, as I have intimated, it could be any type of group or cluster of thought, such as jealousy, depression, frustration and many others that would be stored as a big, ugly sponge waiting to deposit them upon you consciously.

A more interesting group would be those that would be more hidden that would cause someting like tiredness or low energy. Has this ever happened to you?

*"That's why we're so late getting started working on the book today. I had to have a nap first."*

Would you like to find out what was behind this?

*"I really would."*

(Seth conducts an experiment.)

All right. The experiment appears to have been successful. I started off with "tiredness" and you responded with what?

*"Depression."*

"Black energy."

*"Orange."*

"Underlying."

*"Avoiding."*

What was involved here was that you were avoiding the solution. You wished to avoid doing some research work concerning this book. John said he would do it for you, but later. Identifying with a particular being who was in your house today, who had similar thought trains, caused you to go into a pattern of tiredness and a nap to avoid what your ego thought would be an unpleasant task. In this case, avoidance equals tiredness. The task itself now may appear a little differently to you. Is that correct?

*"Yes, I'm looking forward to it."*

Feeling more energized now?

*"Yes."*

It is important to delineate these hidden patterns or groups of thought as they arise to illustrate what I am attempting to teach, to unravel the thought process that would be in control of you, not you in control of it. When someting is in control of you, it can clearly make you tired and you have not the slightest notion of where it stems.

Now, thought is grouped in another more interesting way. Let us say that someone would start explaining a process to you. This process is one that would involve you in a new undertaking. (Not associated with undertaking.) This new venture might be one that would lead you into a different way of being or mode of living. Someone would start explaining this process to you. The being explaining it has certain experiences along the lines of the new venture which would be quite helpful to you. Their talents are such that they could lead you around certain problems. After a lengthy explanation, details were laid out for future probable plans which would enable you to undertake the new action. All present thought that all had agreed to the same thing. You thought that all were in agreement, also. After a period of time, you discovered that maybe you were left out. Somehow, your pattern of thought was such that the message conveyed was different than all experience would suggest. Does this sound familiar?

*"Too familiar."*

What has happened here?

*"Quite frequently, somebody says something and I hear something else."*

This happens all too frequently with communication of thoughts between beings. You might use what would seem to be a perfectly natural tone of voice to convey a message. John might hear it as something offensive to him. Again, what is going on here? It is simple. You have a particular connected group of thought that would convey a message to you that would be tied in to past experience and not to the present or now moment. You would associate that which was said to a meaning that was no longer true. You would associate now thought with past thought which would be like adding a plus one and a negative one and arriving at nothing. What this means is, and many beings attach to this grouping, to associate the present with the past and come up with a false grouping of thought. If one would take what is said in the now moment now and avoid mixing the thought with false or past experience, then the message conveyed in the now moment would remain fact. Do you understand?

*"Somebody says something and it triggers fear because you hear it as a warning. You don't want to hear it as a warning because you don't want to think it would happen to you. So you push it under the surface, but you're afraid. It causes a memory of somebody in the past giving you a warning and you found out it was true later and you were hurt."*

Now, all experience in each and every now moment is unique unto itself. What this means is, if one could disconnect the past experience or thought or group of thoughts from the now moment and treat it as it is, then one would not hear from fear. When you hear from fear, you are not hearing from the now moment, but are hearing from the past which would automatically become the future. The association of this group of thoughts would now take control and project it into the future, making an automatic decision resulting in fear which then becomes automatically false, robbing you of the true experience. What is interesting here is that each thought is unique unto itself and each thought would have a solution that is also unique unto itself. The ego makes the error of comparing experience to the past instead of remaining open to the present. This may not be clear yet, but what I am saying here is that each new thought, regardless of how it would appear to be exactly like an old thought, would require the use of intuition for a solution, not association from the past.

Now, higher thought not only is faster with the solution, but would not be limited or harnessed to old or false solutions. The ego is limited to its experience whereby the higher intelligence is open and not limited to the experience of the ego. What I am say-ing is that the higher self adds to but is not limited to experience from the past. Each event then is unique unto itself. I do not wish to wear this out, but it is important to use your seeing eye, not your limited one.

Beings have fixed trains or groups of thought which play out old solutions to new problems, making new problems temporarily unsolvable. I do not wish to confuse the issue here by having it seem that a word would trigger a control variable and spout out an experience. The difference with the group of thought would necessarily imply that the group of experience thought would be different from that of a controlled variable.

For simplicity, then, we would call this experience groups. Now, how would you disconnect the now moment from an ex-perience group?

*"That's what I was going to ask you."*

I have a few examples that may help with this process. What if you saw someone who looked like someone you knew and you met him at a store? Would you expect him to act in a certain way?

*"Yes, I'd expect his regular personality."*

But if it only looked like the person you knew and it wasn't the same being, would you then be surprised if he acted differently?

*"No."*

Good. Because this is exactly the way that each new event need be brought into focus to warrant its inclusion as a new situation.

Let us take a carpenter who would be hanging doors of all the same size, one after the other, for some time. All of a sudden, on a rainy day, he would find one that did not fit. The carpenter forgot something. Do you know what it is?

*"He forgot that when it rains, the wood might swell."*

Again, each situation is unique, no matter how it looks. A salesman might come to your door and your image of salesmen is, get rid of them, and so you do. A week later, your neighbor in-forms you of a unique, new idea that saved him several hours per week with a particular job. This information was sold to him by the salesman whom you associated with all other salesmen. When you attempted to reach this salesman, he had left your area and was no longer available. Again, different situation, same point.

There is a solution to this dilemma. If one could focus in the now moment, then intuition would automatically come into play and bring in the solution more swiftly than a speeding train. Is this too simple?

*"I don't think so. It's mostly a matter of having the courage to test it out."*

One need exercise one's intuition to isolate current information from past influences. When information is processed in the now moment, one need isolate where the solution is raised. When someone exchanges information with another being, if one suspects that pressure from the past is influencing current solutions, then the following action can be taken. As you are speaking with another, try to focus on some object that he is wearing, such as a button on a shirt or blouse. In the absence of this, one could focus on a pocket, a tie, a ring or some other object. I think that will clarify the idea. This is to say that you don't focus your whole attention on the object in question that you select, but just be aware that that object exists in the now moment. Let us try something here.

(Seth conducts an experiment.)

Now, when you selected a button on John's shirt, that was easy to focus on, wasn't it?

*"Yes."*

When I brought up the subject of your father and spoke of him playing music on his trumpet, it wasn't too difficult to focus on the button, was it?

*"No."*

He didn't play the trumpet around you. Now, when I asked you about playing music in general, then your attention began to wander and you defocused from the button and were unable to stay in the now moment. Is that correct?

*"That's correct."*

This would illustrate a powerful point, if you could but control it. Beings start to speak with you and pictures are formed out of the past, coloring your judgment in a way that would sway your mood, generally in an unhappy way. When thoughts are entertained in this fashion, groups of thought from the past then take control. An alteration of your mood is then effected. Beings are quite unaware of these influences and much difficulty in their lives could be avoided if they could disconnect from these influences.

Let us take an example from the other day, of where you were not getting the point. If you could then focus on an object at these times, it would circumvent some of these problems. Were you aware at the time that others thought differently than you did?

*"You want to know exactly what went through my head at the time?"*

Yes.

*"I thought that the subject was so threatening to me that I just left the now moment. I reverted back to past behavior to combat the threat, seeking not to let them know in any way that I was threatened. The rest of the conversation was meaningless to me. My sole concern was not to reveal that I was disturbed. I then proceeded to deal with my own fears and could not have others helping me out."*

This happens ever so frequently with beings intersecting with other beings. The conversation starts, something is triggered and then the balance of the conversation is lost. This can be so strong that when one would ask about such a conversation, you would believe it different from what the other beings said and what others around you hear. It would be so strong that the total meaning would be lost. This happens to salesmen and they lose the order because they lost their concentration in the now moment. This happens with doctors who start to convey their analysis of disease and their first few words are so threatening that the balance of the explanation which would defuse the first few words, would be totally lost. It happens to lawyers, business-men, secretaries and in every walk of life, causing confusion and, at times, disease.

How many times has a couple started out seeking to resolve a conflict and the same old group of thought would be replayed in such a manner that they might as well record it once and be done with it? That is to say, a conversation between the couple can start with any thought and then the fuse is lit, bringing in stan-dard groups of thoughts. They might just as well turn on a record and let the balance of the conversation take care of itself without either being in the room. Do you know what I mean?

*"I really identify with this."*

Now, as I have spoken, there are ways of getting out of this problem. John would seek to always use a different approach toward conveying the same information. For example, if you are to go someplace, in order to communicate the proper time to leave, he uses many different means, not the same old subject, such as, "It is time to go." He might have one of the children convey the message or send in the dog with a note or play the piano or call you on the telephone. But I think you get the idea. What I am saying here is, one can live an ordinary life in a non-ordinary way, seeking to make the most mundane of matters interesting. What effect might this have?

*"It keeps things from getting boring."*

You are trying to guess what I am thinking. What I am thinking is, it is never boring in the now moment.

This is an interesting technique we are discussing, because it serves to illustrate the point so well. By constantly shifting your point of focus in the now moment, seeking to make every event new and fresh, the old patterns or groups of thought are not used to control your thinking. Do you know what I mean by this?

*"I think it would be like being a child again. Everything would be more fun."*

Beings allow themselves to form their lives along certain patterns or groups of thought. If one is not careful, everything becomes routine, dull or boring. With a little effort, different events can be scheduled a little differently in time, allowing flexibility, which will result in the most mundane of chores appearing interesting.

Now, we are into routine, aren't we?

*"Yuk!"*

Do you have a routine?

*"I tried to keep a routine all my life and was never successful. Now there is no routine to our lives. We do whatever is to be done when it comes up and that changes daily. The problem is that I feel guilty at not having a routine, which I always hated, anyway."*

Now, if one is interested in what is taking place in one's life, then the concept of routine patterns of thought becomes less important. One of the problems, it seems to me, with the current state of events, is that the lives of so many beings are in such

structured routines that they become very glum and boring.
With but little effort, these groups of thought can be broken in
such a way as to bring the focus into the now moment where
everything is interesting. Now, I am not saying that the world in
its present state need be restructured in such a way that one
would become unstructured, interferring with the lives of other
beings.

Now, your life, which you felt the guilt of being unstructured,
would then take on another meaning which would be the reverse
of what you thought. Think of those times of your life where you
have been most happy. Would these times be structured?

*"Absolutely not."*

How would this be?

*"My jobs have been such that I've made my own schedule,
which changed daily."*

This is not to say, again, that one would rebel and change the
world. When one would seek to have a more interesting life, it
would seem the more one would vary his routine way of thinking,
the more exercised would be his use of the greater or intuitive
self. Starting to practice using the intuitive self to guide one's
daily routine would serve to restructure the routine into a non-
routine. Pick something that you hate to do.

*"That's easy. I am supposed to fix the kids' lunches every
morning."*

How were you and John able to get around this problem?

*"We take turns."*

What would happen if you got tired of that routine?

*"We'd have them buy lunches at school or let them come home
for lunch."*

With each routine in your life, it would be interesting to break
the routine by using insight to light a new path to keep your interest from waning. When you would start to restructure your life
in this way, in no time would you find that your imagination
would start coming out, inventing even newer ways to make your
life more meaningful and interesting. When you focus in this
manner, it opens the door for every new creative energy to seek
you out, filling your life with new insight, further stimulating you
out of stale groups of thought which would influence your mood
in a negative fashion and rob you of energy.

It would be interesting for all those reading this book to make a list of all the routines in their lives. After looking at this list, for an interesting exercise, try to change some of your routine, whether it be the time it is done, or inventing new ways to accomplish the same routine with different insight. You need not make the list too long, but just try to change it a little bit. It would be to the surprise of no one that in but a short time, your life suddenly took on new meaning. And, yes, I do mean this technique is quite powerful. When a being becomes dull and boring or over-routinized, life becomes not worth living.

Now, who might be the most unstructured individual that you might ever meet?

*"A hobo, or a master."*

I wasn't thinking of a hobo, but you do have a good point. They seem to get on with their lives without benefit of a time clock, but something would be a little amiss here in that there is some discomfort. Where there is discomfort, then one would suspect that one might have ego, which is never in the now moment. Now, the master would not be in the ego and being a master, he would have mastered his routines. Now, the master is not unfamiliar with routines, otherwise, he would not know them and could not master them. He would be one who would have overcome the need for routine. What would then replace it? Do you know?

*"Going with the flow."*

Yes. Staying in the now moment would automatically put him in touch with the flow and his life would be routinized automatically for him, which would be no routine at all. So you may be heading in the right direction, after all. Guilt, then, is really something false, again, isn't it? Can you think of other groups of thought?

*"Not offhand."*

Would you take the word "habit" to be any different than routine? The only way I would differentiate in my way of viewing them would be to have routine be a more blatant course of action whereby habit would be less conscious and of smaller consequence. Would you agree with this?

*"Totally. Habits are milder, not so noticeable."*

As is known by some, it takes about twenty-one days to break a habit. Habits can be ways of brushing your hair, dressing, driving a certain route to work. With a little effort, even these habits could be changed once in a while to help you remain in the now moment. It would be surprising with adding different colors around you, different music or maybe even engaging in conversation, how these habits would take on new meaning. So, even exploring the most mundane levels of existence could open you up in ways that you would not foresee.

Remember when a friend of yours suggested that you sleep on the other side of the bed? What happened? It changed your mode of behavior. Why didn't you continue this?

*"I wasn't used to it."*

Well, I'll let you get away with that and not push the issue. But you can see the point, in any event.

Becoming aware of, first of all, groups of thought and then becoming aware that they are controlling you, making your existence dull and boring, would seem to be sufficient impetus to bring about willingness to start using your intuition for happiness.

# CHAPTER 7

## INTERRELATIONSHIPS OF THOUGHT

If one thought about it, one might think one thought begets another. One thought might relate to another, in other words. Now, there are keys to these words that go far beyond what is printed here. Let us say that you have an entrenched pattern of guilt. This might have been in place for many years. Now, let us say that this particular group of entrenched thoughts was placed there in such a way that it was placed in others, also. Let us say that this worn groove of thought was so strong that it, in effect, was deposited in others, also.

Now, when your son, Johnny, was four years old, something happened, didn't it?

"*Yes.*"

And what was that? For various reasons, Johnny was left alone a good share of the time. This went on for a period of months. This led to guilt on your part and withdrawal on his, which put in guilt on his part and withdrawal on yours. So, this led to a pattern of behavior on both of your parts which served to put a wall between you, didn't it?

"*Yes.*"

Now, what you didn't know was that your guilt thought was not only entrenched within your subconscious, but within his, also. But in his subconscious, not readily indentifiable as guilt.

Now, in a previous chapter, when I asked you to hand me all of your guilt, did you do so?

*"Yes."*

What you didn't realize was that you handed something else to me, didn't you?

*"No."*

What you handed me was his share of the guilt that you installed within him. This seems utterly fantastic, doesn't it?

*"Yes."*

Now, how could this be?

*"I don't know."*

(Seth lights a cigarette and shows me the Irish Jig, from one of his past incarnations.)

What happens in the NOW MOMENT, (Seth gets very strong,) is that you then change the past and the probable future, for all there is is now. Very powerful. In other words, that which was, now isn't. That which is, was, also. Do you understand?

*"Did what happened actually change the past experience that Johnny and I had?"*

Yes. Is not Johnny different now?

*"Quite different."*

Literally overnight. You placed your thought within him. Since you have placed it there, then you have the right to change it. (Seth smiles at this.) So changing this in the now moment changes the interrelationships between your thoughts and his. It triggers the code in both, doesn't it? The interesting part of this is, it is changed in every incarnation, also. Now, what did I do? Obviously, since nothing is lost, I have somehow enabled you to change energy to convert the thought into something else. The something else would, of course, be another form of energy, for nothing is ever wasted, is it? When this thought is then removed and there is a lot of it, then it creates a vacuum. Something will then fill it. Initially, it is sadness if there is a lot of it, which there was. But in no time, something will fill it and it might be to your greatest benefit.

Now, when you handed this to me, I somehow knew that you were holding some of it back, didn't I? Did you know it then, also?

(Seth kept asking me to hand over my guilt willingly until I gave it all to him.)

By connecting to the affected area, it caused an opening for it to flow out, you see. This works with all beings. By carefully entrusting me with it, and I was careful to say that I would give it back if you liked it, did I not? You then handed it all to me. Very nice of you.

(Seth races across the room.)

I then held it up to the sun which was a symbol of transforming the pile of energy. It could be light or any form of energy. Did you know that it had changed the energy form at the time?

*"No, I was very confused the whole time this was taking place and did not realize what you were doing."*

Now, when you entrusted me with your guilt, you allowed its removal. You allowed it to be placed aside, hence, its removal.

Now, do you know what? If you can do this with your very largest and longest lasting problem, could you imagine the same with any other problem?

*"Yes."*

All thoughts are interrelated. Furthermore, those which are changed and within others, originating from you, are also changed . . . in the now moment.

What do you think would happen to your sphere of influence?

*"I think it would grow larger."*

Yes. And something of it would change. As you would then influence others, this particular aspect of guilt would not "bump into others," would it?

*"No."*

How do you think the outer sphere ties in with the inner sphere?

*"I don't know."*

You have seen a cloud emitted from a being's head that would depict a sphere of influence, haven't you? Was it about twenty feet wide?

*"Yes."*

All right. Was it about a foot and a half to two feet thick?

*"Yes."*

I thought so, Now, there must have been some kind of connecting link between the outer and the inner, wouldn't you think?

*"Yes."*

That sphere is what the being is in this incarnation, is it not? What do you think this sphere is composed of, then?

*"His energy or thought."*

Where do you think your thoughts would be stored?

*"I don't know."*

Would they be in the mind?

*"Yes."*

What is the mind? Do you know?

*"I don't think I do."*

The mind is but this sphere of influence, isn't it? Of course, no one knows this. But it is a mere storehouse of thought and a processing unit.

(Seth has just conducted another experiment involving guilt.)

Now, this one had a different feeling to it than the first, didn't it?

*"Yes. There is no feeling of sadness or loss."*

Do you have any idea why?

*"No."*

This experiment involved an emotional hue that was a different association of thought than the other. Do you know why?

*"No."*

This was an area that is basically all right with you, under the right condition. Then the behavior is basically all right without the underlying, interrelated thought put into you by others. Do you understand now?

*"Yes, I do."*

You cannot live others' value systems in your own life without getting into troubled waters. Erasing the thought put upon you by others removed the guilt in a manner that would correct the imbalance in you.

Now, what did I mean by emotional hue, in reference to your sphere of influence? Each group of interrelated thought has a particular color or hue to it which pervades your whole sphere of influence.

Now, of course, the sphere of influence is circular. You did know that, did you not?

*"I saw it as a band of color projecting outward from a person's head, about ten feet on each side. But I didn't see it as circular."*

Well, I'm glad we cleared that up, for it is indeed circular. Did the sphere of influence appear different from one being to the next?

*"Yes. On one being, the sphere was higher on one side than on the other side."*

Was this consistent with what John saw?

*"Yes. He saw the same thing I did. I think there was an imbalance in the second person."*

Indeed. Did they appear to speak in colors?

*"Yes. As I watched the person who was on stage, speaking to a large group, a band of color formed, going through the person's head and extending to a distance of about ten feet on each side of the head. Then brilliant colors began flashing all over. As the color became stronger, I could no longer hear the words being spoken. I was overtaken by the colors. The people on the stage, the podium, the stage curtains and all the people in the audience became colors. I eventually shook my head to clear it because as this color became more intense, it appeared to me that the room tilted. The stage and everything on it tilted sideways."*

Now, this is an area not readily understood. When one speaks with an emotional hue, many factors come into play. One's communication is colored, so to speak. One's combination of thought is colored in a way that brings his message to another with a certain degree of understanding placed there by their feeling in the now moment. This, perhaps, is the most mystifying aspect of beinghood. What are we, as beings? We are, in the now moment, all of the emotionally charged thought that is the sum total of our existence. Thought is so powerful that if a particularly strongly implaced charged thought places its influence in the surrounding sphere, all of those within its influence will be influenced to the degree that it interconnects with their particularly charged thought.

Now, think of the ramifications of this.

*"The sphere is the sum total of all of the experience we have ever been in the now moment."*

Each sphere intersects with another sphere, each influencing the other. Now, within each sphere are what we would call thought particles. In between the thought particles is something we, again, would call *stuff*. The *stuff* is the coloration which the sphere will then contain. Let us say, on a given day, someone will have more anger than at another given time. The *stuff* will take on the color spectrum in the lower or darker area and will have an effect on the whole sphere. The interconnecting link of the individual thought particle is the *stuff.* Beings then speak in colors, you see. Understand that the spoken word is but a minute part of communication, somewhat less than one could think. Have you ever wondered why a speaker would speak using certain exact words and your feeling would be "ho-hum?" Then another speaker would get up, speaking the same exact words and you would take on the feeling of exhilaration. Beings, with use of language, fall short in their ability to describe this function. So, I now will attempt to describe adequately how this function works.

Let us say that you have a clear glass of water. You then add a drop of red food coloring. What would happen?

*"The water would turn red."*

How would it turn red? Would it turn red slowly?

*"The drop would hit and it would slowly change the color of the water."*

You might even need to stir it a little. This generally would follow the pattern of most coloration of thought with the sphere. Now, let us say that the water was already being stirred prior to the dropping of the red food coloring. What do you think would happen now?

*"The water would change color faster."*

Yes. That's what I thought. The amount of energy placed within the thought is directly dependent on how rapidly the change in coloration of thought within this sphere will be influenced. For example, if one thought, "It is a nice day," then the coloration would slowly be mixed with the hue of this thought. Now, if one were burdened with guilt and guilt were triggered, then the charge would rapidly color the hue of the sphere and the charge would be more overpowering or rapid. That is, if the charged thought were already grouped in abundance and there was a large potential, then but a small trigger would ignite a fire. Do you understand this? Now, if one thought, "It is a nice day and I should be out enjoying it," then guilt would color the hue more rapidly.

Now, if each being is the sum total of all his thoughts, then this must necessarily also include hues. So, now we have thoughts and hues. Did you know that it was so much easier to discuss thought in color?

*"I can see that. If I think, 'That person is the sum total of every thought and experience he has ever been,' I still don't have much understanding of that person. But if I look at a person and see a pleasant color coming out of his head, then I know why I am so attracted to that person."*

Now, some feel, some see. What is the difference?

(Now Seth conducts an experiment.)

*"Oh, my God!"*

Don't worry.

Now, when in this experiment, I closed the shade and shined the light on my (John's) face, there was a switch in your feeling, wasn't there?

*"Yes."*

And that switch was due to a change in light, was it not? Did not the light bring in a more intimate feeling?

*"Yes, it did."*

Was this the same feeling as if John would playfully face you eyeball to eyeball?

*"Yes, it was."*

What did I do there?

*"I don't understand how that worked, but it had the effect of me seeing John differently than I normally do."*

You saw him in a different light. What does this say? If you change the lighting in a certain way, then you change the interrelationship of feeling. Have I not proven that thought is light? And light is energy. Are you convinced of this?

*"I know this is true. I just experienced it."*

I could take this coat and put it over his head and you would have a diffrent feeling again. Is that not so?

*"I don't know. Let me see you do it."*

(Seth puts the coat over John's head.)

*"It's definitely a different feeling."*

I believe you are convinced now. Who is John? John is a collection of light and energy which you would describe as thought, also. Yes?

*"Yes."*

Now, what are friends, in this light? Friends are the matching of interconnecting thought in a way that many thoughts are quite similar and this would be of what is called the same vibration or the same energy or the same thought.

Now, let us get back to our speaker. As the speaker speaks, certain colors or light energy are emitted by the thousands. When there is a cohesion of a projected particle with that of the listener, then those particular particles interconnect forming a bond changing both. Now, as these two particles would interconnect, then the merged energy of both separate thoughts form a new energy that has a new charge. Now, another listener hearing the same thought particle would also have a cohesive bond forming a new charged thought that would be different than the charge of the first listener, depending on the emotional charge registering in both the second listener and the speaker. Each would hear the same words but would receive different messages depending upon their emotional charge.

Going back to our experiment with the flashlight. As the light around the head changed, so in turn, the feeling about the subject being changed, also. Isn't that right?

*"Yes, it is."*

Now, this would tend to show that the amount of light emitted by a being and received by another would be directly proportional to the amount of charge received. Now, what this means is that the message received is due to the amount of light. Now, what does all of this mean? Have you any idea?

*"Vaguely."*

Okay. Now, the charge of the emotion or thought received is directly proportional to the vibrational influence. That is, the light that is receivable is the thought energy that is capable of being heard. To explain further: If a so-called master were speaking to a group, each would know the transcribed thought energy to the degree that he was capable of knowing it. Notice the idea is postulated that those in the light only seem to intersect those of like kind who are able to intersect the transcribed thought. The reference to color or light is important to understand the inter-relationship of the transference of thought energy between beings in proportion to the light of understanding.

Now, each thought, then, has its own light velocity. Why, for instance, would something of new technology be invented at several places at the same time? If the new idea was one of higher, lighter velocity or intelligence, then it would be faster and have a greater range. Beings, then, in their growth, would become lighter and of a higher vibration, able to receive and transmit thought energy of a higher, lighter kind, disposing them into a larger and larger sphere of influence.

Now, let us take a sphere of influence which is growing rapidly. The influence of the sphere is of a nature that, as the heavier, darker ego characteristics are changed or forgiven, then the sphere changes composition. The sphere then becomes lighter in color, in weight, would become larger and conduction is predisposed to higher and higher thought. The charge is, of course, of less an emotional nature but more magnetic in character. It thus becomes axiomatic that one's association or friends change as elevation occurs. The influence of heavier thought or thought of an emotional nature becomes less and less. The influence of truth or higher thought increasingly adds to the attractiveness of the sphere, enabling those possessed of this to appear magnetic.

(Seth leaves the room, skipping. He conducts another experiment.)

An amazing experiment!

"I closed my eyes and Seth came into the room, I felt. Seth then asked me to feel how he felt from a distance. Seth then left the room again and came back. My eyes were still closed. He asked, again, how he felt and I said, 'More serious.' I had a vision of a pyramid with the left side dropped. It was not a good feeling. He again asked how he felt and I said, 'Sideways,' and I saw a pyramid that was open sideways. He again asked how he felt and I said, 'More direct,' and I saw a pyramid that was open to me. I said, 'You feel more direct.' Seth then asked me to open my eyes and I saw that he had placed a piece of copper and a quartz crystal in front of me."

Now, what have I done? I didn't change my energy. I changed the coloration or mood mechanically between you and me. You felt that I had changed mood or energy when I only put in a filter and changed it mechanically. What have I demonstrated?

"You mechanically changed moods or color."

Now, do you think that if I could do this, you could do this?

"Absolutely. After I learn how."

This is what the speaker actually accomplished. The interrelationship between the mood of the speaker and those listening actually provided the new cohesive thought. You have done this, yourself. Have you ever noticed that when you are in a great or good mood, that nothing stands in your way to diminish the good feeling?

*"Yes."*

Now, in light of what we have discussed so far, it is readily apparent that the pervading mood exuded would be that of the speaker. I have shown that this could be changed by use of a crystal and a device such as a piece of copper. Now then, the trick would be how to put forth a consistent message flowing with a graceful energy each time. Now, do you have any idea of how to do this?

*"I don't think one can 'do' this. I think one has to 'be' this."*

You are half right. Now then, how do you change who you are to be? How do you know who you are at a given now moment?

*"By how you feel."*

Yes. Now, how does one reconstruct a mood, a whim, something that is underneath the surface that drives one? When one would learn to control his thoughts, then the control of mood would be automatic, wouldn't it? However, before one can control his thoughts, a number of interconnecting links need be understood.

One of those links is how implanted thought is connected between involved beings. Now, if sometime in the past, something was buried within two or more beings, again the degree of its implantation would be directly proportional to the emotional charge.

Now, there must be some way that these thoughts still are connected, wouldn't you think?

*"I suspect there is a way."*

Yes, indeed. A situation came up today where someone out of the past triggered a memory out of the past. Since both were involved, then the thought must have somehow been interconnected. Little silver threads that go out in every direction connecting those thoughts, when triggered in one, would trigger in the other. The chord would be resonated, triggering or bringing up the thought in proportion to the emotional charge placed there by each. Both might react. Now, let us say that a couple kept getting into the same emotional argument over and over and it got worse and worse until nearly any word might trigger the same argument. Now, how could this be? The grooves are worn, the strings are pulled and the same argument is then started again. For it could not stop unless one or the other rooted out the entrenched group of thoughts. Now, what does the expression mean, "He pulled my string"? Have you ever heard this?

*"Yes, I've heard it and I've had it happen to me."*

Did you know that your strings were being pulled?

*"Yes, but by the time I realized it, it was too late to pull out of it because I was too caught up in the emotionalism."*

What does "pulling strings" mean? Maybe someone was quite clever in picking this up. The figure of speech was put forth by someone who imagined thoughts were connected in this fashion, wasn't it? Now, if two or more thoughts are connected by strings, obviously they do not sit forth as islands to themselves, locked away from any other trigger or interaction. Now, when the speaker we spoke of would speak a line, would this not strike but one of the responsive chords? Let us then take a few examples.

The speaker speaks a word and the word, whatever it is, strikes a chord and all of a sudden, you are thinking you are fat. The speaker speaks another word, again whatever it is, and suddenly your right arm aches. But another word and you think how nice your mother was. Now, it is evident by this time that this is true, is it now?

*"Yes, it is."*

Now, the chords come into play, so to speak, don't they? When you would unsuspectingly hear anything, it might trigger any of a variety of responses. And the information would be channeled through the right series of pathways into your coded storage place. With then the correct use of certain words, one could then associate to a certain storage place and bring out literally anything stored there, with the free choice of the one wishing to bring out some area of thought.

(Seth then holds up his finger as a signal to stop.)

Now, each chord then would have a frequency or vibrational level, would it not? Then if this were the case, some might resonate at a particular response to a certain word and others would not. Take the word "thing" for instance.

If I say the word "thing" what would you think of?

*"Event."*

Someone else might think of a possession, such as a car, a spider or any number of things. Why would you associate "thing" with an event, for instance?

*"I don't know. The word 'event' came into my head when you said 'thing'."*

Okay. That is your particular coding mechanism for your sphere. Now, I'm going to bring John back and you ask him the same thing and see what his response is. "Thing."

*John: "Stop."*

Now, that is his coding process, isn't it? I know you're wondering what this means, aren't you?

*"Yes, I am. It seems like an odd response to me."*

What it meant was, this particular word "thing" would be as a stopper or a blocking mechanism. Do you understand? I will explain further. If you wish to go on to some subject that with his willingness would wish to be unearthed, then you would say "green" and then he would say "go."

So, as you see, there is a myriad of words, colorations and feelings known as thought, hitting responsive chords, triggering a chain into a specific location which would bring out a thought, coloring your moods or feelings at any given moment. Now you can see that many colorations of influence would send your life in many directions at any given now moment. (Humorously.) Think of the ramifications of this. Let us say you are walking into a store and you hear the word "sheep," and all of a sudden, you are visiting a sheep ranch in Montana. Depending upon the emotional charge of the word "sheep" in your sphere, the coloration or mood would influence your thoughts for the next few seconds or hours. Do you feel this?

*"Yes. Many times, as I sit and talk to someone, I suddenly am off on my own trip."*

Notice the response to that particular group of words, taken from your sphere. Now, if someone accidently said the "right" or "wrong" word or series of words, it could ruin your day. There are those who have the power and have somehow learned to direct energy in a way that would influence the thought of others. They would seek to control the thought of others. Let us take those

who would hypnotize you. If you were willing enough and sufficient good purpose were in evidence, then the result would influence future probable behavior for a period of time. If one was
brainwashed sufficiently to drive an emotionally charged thought
deep enough, then the behavior would become automatic until the
behavior was removed. Now, how would this be done? One thing
comes to mind, of course. One could remove it in the same way it
was placed there. This would be rather painful, wouldn't it? Fortunately, there is at least one other way. If one knew the code or
the key to find where the behavior pattern or thought pattern
could be located, then one could expose it and facilitate its
removal. This is part of what I propose to teach. The forced inges-
tion of this technique is heinous in method. Understanding in
word picture form how the thought pattern was placed there, of
course, is the key to its coded removal. Naturally, then, the person or persons placing it there are connected with its removal.
Also, the surroundings and the feelings with it are instrumental
in understanding the coded method in which it was implaced.
This is not so different as one might imagine if it could be compared to the way all learned behavior patterns were placed in the
sphere.

Let us use a little example of this. When you were five years
old, your father would ask you to pick up an object off the floor
and place it in its proper place. Now, if he asked you in a very
strong way, perhaps you would do it. Is this not so?

"*Yes.*"

The strength of the feeling placed in the request could initially
bring you to respond in an unemotional way. If the strength of
the request were quite strong, it would then bring in other
thoughts. A few names of unprintable character might come to
mind. Other thoughts might also come in about a similar situation a year prior to this or some past association of behavior. If
the individual making the request was directly tied to some emotionally charged event in the past, then all kinds of thought erup-
tion, and I use this to denote mood, could take place

Now, initially, when I mentioned the word "brainwash," certain things came to mind. The first was your fascination with it,
then your isolation and withdrawal with it. This word then triggered a whole series of events over two days for you and John,

didn't it?

*"Yes, it did."*

Now then, these events started with a reaction from you, somehow coincidentally drawing in another couple. The phone rings and the next thing you know, the other couple is then discussing a major difference of opinion or experience that you and John needed to work out. This one word then opened up all kinds of pictures and events tied to the ramifications of it. It then became necessary for all kinds of sphere searching to unlock some areas of strong emotional response in the two of you which had the effect of a continuing game which needed to be cleared up so the two of you could then work more efficiently together. Do you see the interrelationship here of thought, strong emotion and a whole series of interrelating events bringing in others, to map out unresolved areas of emotional thought that were hidden from your conscious understanding of the stress?

*"I understand it completely because I just experienced it."*

Now, what I am teaching you, example by example, and you are indeed living it, is a method of understanding how emotionally charged thoughts are interrelated in a manner that you would not suspect.

Now, imagine again the powerful effect of any conscious trigger or words that you would experience on any given day.

(All of sudden, Seth switches gears, becomes more active. Seth conducts another experiment.)

Now, I was just informing you that all of a sudden, your whole family seems quite happy. Now, when I picked up these rods (divining rods) and walked over to the dog with them, the dog had a certain degree of energy, as measured by the divining rods opening up as I approached the dog. Now, do you know what I am going to do?

*"I am not certain of what took place here."*

I am showing you how thought changes your energy. When I walked to the dog, I stopped when the rods opened up. Did you notice that when I spoke to the dog and its tail wagged, the rods opened up further?

*"Yes, that's what I saw."*

When the dog then lay down and quieted, the rods receded or started to close up. When I next spoke to the dog and it was a friendly gesture on my part, the rods again opened up. What I have done here is measure and demonstrate to you that the feeling, thought or emotional hue could be measured, depending on its response to my overtures to her. What have I just proven to you?

*"You gave the dog attention which made her happy and increased her energy, causing the rods to open further."*

So I have now proven to you that thought energy exists, have I not? Now, this was a dog, a friendly one with no ego resistance. Do you think one would see the same sort of response in beings?

*"Sometimes, but not in most beings."*

Would you be able to see this with John, without me present?

*"Certainly."*

Yes.

*(I handed the rods to my son, Johnny, and there was a certain resistance to believing what he was seeing. The rods were moving, but he insisted that he was making them move.)*

What does this show you?

*"It shows me that if a person is open, anything is possible. If the mind is closed, nothing is possible."*

This experiment sheds new energy on things, doesn't it? Seeing this with the dog would seem to prove that by *giving* others attention, their energy increases. The higher energy, as we again proved, is the happier or love energy, as the dog showed. When you give others love energy or attention, then their energy increases. Now, this doesn't have to be in the form of words, either. If I could measure it and use John's body at the same time, to pet the dog, what do you think the dog's response would be with the divining rods?

*"The rods would open wider."*

Yes. Now, what if I looked at the dog and thought, "How nice you are, how friendly you are." Do you think the rods would react?

*"They would react exactly the same as if the words had been spoken."*

Yes. Do you think that this would work in the same way with beings?

*"I think that the thought is more effective than the spoken words. If I see a friend and admire her new hairstyle, I might ap-*

*proach her and say I like the new hairstyle, that she looks terrific.
The words might be accepted or they might not. The person
might respond, 'Oh, thank you, but I just hate it.' They can block
out my words easily by their preconceived opinion. But if I genu-
inely like it, they will receive the thought and feel happy, even
though they refuse to hear the words. On the other hand, if I see a
friend and think, 'What did she do to her hair! It looks terrible,'
she will get that message along with the spoken words, 'Your hair
looks terrific,' and she will feel confused and uncomfortable."*

Now, with an animal, especially a dog, the feelings or thought
are quite simple. There is nothing in the way. When the thought
is put out, the dog gets the direct message. Have you ever noticed
that when you look at a dog, if it is a stern look, the dog would
stop what it is doing? When it is a loving look, the dog responds
to you in a friendly manner. Now, beings are a little different, for
it is rare that the false personality, known as the ego, is not in the
way. If you would have a stern enough look with no feeling
behind it, how do you think you might take it?

*(Seth gives me a stern look. The eyes become very serious and
the face is set.)*

*"That's very strange."*

How was it that it was strange?

*"The look was there, a look I would normally have a strong
reaction to, but there was no reaction and I feel confused."*

Yes. It's interesting, isn't it?

*"Very interesting. I could have a lot of fun with this. If I could
perfect this, I could walk up to a person and say, 'You are full of
it,' and if I had a happy, friendly feeling about him at the time, he
might say, 'Thank you, it's nice to see you'."*

Yes. Now, when you learn how, you can project any mood, feeling or thought that you would desire! In a simplistic manner, I
have shown you a reduced energy, stern look. This is not so easy
to convey to another being, however, for the other being might
have a responsive chord tied to a group of thought that anyone
who looks sternly, without feeling, is a psychopath, and then we
would have trouble, wouldn't we? So, interrelated thought from
being to being is a more complex matter with which to deal. First,
you see, all manner of projection is taken into account, then all
manner of reception is taken into account and the end result then

becomes fact.

Now, in a related but somewhat different manner, by their very presence, beings' fears can influence all of those around them. Do you think that your family has a collected group of interrelated thought?

*"I never thought about it."*

Your family has certain things in common. The same house, car, food, manner of living, etc. Now, each of these groups of thought is stored and they would have a common chord of connection. All of these thoughts would have a collective group of energy. Now, the collective hue remains in a somewhat balanced state of energy. When a stranger shows up in your house to visit for a few days and the stranger has a lower collection of thought in his sphere, how would you think this would influence your family, especially if you and the stranger had a common group of experiences together?

*"I already know the answer to this because I recently experienced this situation. It had a very negative effect on the entire family."*

Now, as you learned, the stranger didn't even have to be in the same room with you and your family and the effects made a change in your common energy, did it not?

*"We experienced anxiety."*

When he left, the pall or mood stayed around for a little while, didn't it?

*"Yes, it did. It was necessary for all of us to discuss the situation in order to adjust to it."*

After about two days, what happened?

*"John and I realized what was happening and decided that we wanted the person to leave. The person did leave, immediately, without our actually having to say anything."*

The sphere then left and the remaining energy slowly subsided into a new, happier balance.

One could go on and on describing the interrelationship of energy or thought spheres. But those examined would be sufficient to generate an understanding of the interconnecting relationships of spheres, with or without the influence of the spoken word. Time has but little meaning with this influence except in the cataloging effect it has upon the coded storage process within the sphere. (This means that for the mind to keep track of events to retrieve them, a time sequence is used to avoid distortion in a linear world, which is in time, when in actuality, the events are stored in timelessness.)

Note: Thought is then stored in circular, timeless fashion and is then pulled out in a linear order so that the conscious mind can comprehend it and then it is restored in the new block form, back into a sphere or spheres. Thought goes from timelessness to time to timelessness. This book is sitting here in timelessness in a block form. I give it to you in time and then you store it in printed time form and the reader then reads it and stores it in timelessness.

# CHAPTER 8

## NEUTRALIZING THOUGHT

Now, we have taken some pains to describe in detail aspects of thought, storage of thought, its interrelationships and some of its processes. We have examined in a small degree some methods of neutralizing it. Now then, we need get into methods of neutralization in some detail.

Beings have many thoughts throughout a given day that would come to the surface, but only a few would be retained in the limited, conscious memory for immediate processing. The rest would be filed in storage as either being significant or fearful, which could not be handled at the moment they came to the surface.

Now, the insignificant ones might be important, but at the time, they were a solution in search of a problem and the problem had not presented itself. They might be solutions for problems which never quite reach the conscious mind. They might be impressions of someone or something that would not seem to be important or charged in a manner requiring further processing. So little impact or charge is placed with these thoughts that even if a being consciously wished to retrieve them later, it would be quite difficult. How many times have you stated, "I wish I could remember what that was." Does this sound familiar?

*"Yes, it does."*

What would be your most successful method of retrieving these thoughts?

*"I try to remember the approximate time and then try to get a picture of it."*

How successful has this been?

*"Sometimes it works, sometimes it doesn't."*

Would you like a little help with this?

*"Yes."*

If you try your method and it doesn't work, why not try putting the thought into your greater self and asking that the information be revealed to you by tomorrow morning? Do you know what this does?

*"Puts it into the computer."*

Yes, it is put into the greater intelligence computer and it goes to work supplying the requested information. When a being tries too hard to remember something, blocks are put up that stand in the way of retrieving the information. The idea is to neutralize these blocks to greater understanding which will release the information which absolutely is stored. There are those in police work who would hypnotize witnesses to crimes so that the information would be retrieved from the unconscious mind. The subject's willingness and capacity to be hypnotized determines how the information will be released. There have been stories of remarkable success using this method. The idea behind this is to get subjects to relax, out of the ego, so that greater intelligence will take over. Many beings are frustrated constantly, trying to wrestle with such a problem, with little or no success.

Beings are tortured by thought which is just below the surface. You have been an outstanding example of this, which is why you are so valuable a subject, which would help explain some of these concepts. As an outstanding example, it would seem to be relatively easy for other beings to extrapolate what comes from you. Must be a reason you're here.

*"Yes."*

Now, by using coded word association, we have been able to pull out some of these driving forces in your subconscious which would rule your life. We have seen how your dream state will shift your consciousness into your ego in such a way that you would wake up feeling depressed, sad or anxious.

Now, we get into a way of neutralizing dreams. Did my suggested method work for you last night and this morning?

*"Yes, it did."*

Then it worked. This method would be: Prior to going to sleep at night, program yourself to work out one single thing and nothing else in your dream state. That is, to have nothing attached to your instructions to yourself to work out what you would have worked out. Let us say you are getting tired of going to sleep at night in a happy state and waking up anxious. It is a simple matter to program your thought, stating simply, "I will wake up in a happy state in the morning, period." (With emphasis.) Once you have had a recognizable degree of success, confidence builds and you will feel free to attempt solving what you might regard as greater and greater problems. Have you engendered some confidence in this technique?

*"I have a lot of confidence in this technique, because it works for me."*

First comes neutralization of the dream state and then comes the programming to work out problems. If the neutralization is not successful because of lack of practice, then the problem solving will be sporadic, also. This is a larger problem for beings than first meets the eye. Much depression is caused by the hangover effect from dreams that would not necessarily be what the dream was working out. The dream may be quite dark and depressing, but if you could understand it properly, it might be very enlightening. Remember, the ego sees things in reverse. A reoccurring nightmare might be neutralized in this manner. In other words, program it into happiness.

Now, from nightmares, let us go to daymares. Do you know what a daymare is?

*"I think I do. One day I was driving along and I started imagining that something bad might happen to our youngest daughter, Danielle. The feeling got stronger and stronger, but it was only imagination. That happens all the time. It is the feeling of dread in the day, isn't it?"*

Yes, As I have mentioned to you, dreams go on both day and night, or twenty-four hours per day. These dreams need be neutralized, also.

Now, let us say this dread or fear would suddenly surface for no apparent reason. If you would let it go, it would build to a high crescendo, sometimes nearly paralyzing you with fear. Two methods for dealing with this immediately come to mind. The first is to stop, take a deep breath and start working backward to see if you can find the source of this fear. Sometimes, it might be something you have read or a comment from another being. If no solution presents itself, then you might try to capture a feeling of what is being worked out in your conscious, wide awake dream state. Sometimes, it might appear to be more efficient to go on with your day without stopping. This, however, is generally a waste of time, for if you would stop for three minutes and attempt to find the source of this signal, you would then neutralize it, bringing forth happiness. If you bring forth the happy state, remember now, you are more efficient and you will speedily accomplish at least twice as much as you would have had you been in the fear state. *Fear paralyzes; happiness resurrects.* So, we would be benefiting ourselves if we took the time to neutralize the film being shown in the dream state. Imagine a screen as in a movie theatre, in the mind. Motion pictures then are being created and played out. You would stop the projector and seek to edit the production in a manner that would be sufficient for your greater purpose.

Do you understand what I mean by this?

*"Not totally."*

You are getting confused between premonitions, which come from greater thought, and lesser thought, which comes from the ego and would be that of the imagination.

*"Okay, I understand. Another time, Danielle and I were driving along when the clear thought came strongly into my head that I should put the seat belt on her. A minute later, a car pulled in front of me, forcing me to slam on the brakes. There was no fear attached to the thought, just a knowing."*

Yes, that is the difference between imagination and precognition. When there is fear attached, one need suspect that it is only imagination. When there is a strong feeling of knowing, such as the small, little voice gnawing at you, then this would be precognition.

Beings would worry that their dreams and fears would always be precognitive. In actuality, about one in one million is precognitive. One can develop a sense of precognition, but one will be out of the fear state most of the time. Beings will take dream states and believe that it would be an actual state, but it is just working out that which would not be worked out in the physical world. So, you can see that it would be rare that a scene from a dream would actually come into the physical world. Something like that, which would be viewed in a dream, could actually transpire, but it would never, I repeat, never be exactly like the scene depicted in a dream. Now, there have been instances where psychics would predict a disaster from either a dream state or an impression. This would be so rare, however, as to be dismissed unless one began to have a definite track record. Dream states can appear so real as to convince the dreamer that the state or event actually happened. But the dreamer is dreaming only in probable states where the probability is not high.

It is so important to be in a relaxed state when knowing enters into your consciousness that without it, the information projected would be meaningless. Did you know that John has this ability?

*"Yes."*

Precognitive thought is related to intuition. To take advantage of this knowledge, you could make use of it in a way that others need not know. Do you know what I mean?

*"Yes. We don't need to tell everyone that it is going to rain. We just take an umbrella with us."*

What effect would this have, then?

*"It can save us a lot of trouble."*

Yes. It neutralizes the thought.

Now, let us take the dread of future events. Automatically, you know you are in the ego. When this dread appears, let us say, knowing that a particular client will arrive, then one would stop and examine the dread. How many times, you would then ask yourself, has the event worked out as you would fear? In your former business, when you had this fear, at times you could bring the fear into fruition, couldn't you?

*"Yes."*

Either you were in the wrong business for you at that time, which was the case, or you would arrange for the event to come true. Recently, however, have any of these fears come true?

*"No."*

There is a way, of course, that you could have disconnected

these fears, had you known it. If you would but ask for help with this fear, it would indeed be disconnected, wouldn't it?

*"Yes."*

Now, if one of these fears, in the way of someone that you are conversing with, starts to come true, you could neutralize it. Now, this fear, of course, would be one of the person being negative or draining. If the being would start to get into a conversation which would trigger negativity in you, you could then have an etheric silver cord and plug which you could then pull and disconnect when you no longer wished to experience their negativity. The effect of this would be to disconnect the influence of their sphere upon yours with the thought that they intend to use as their influence. They could go on talking, but with the cord disconnected, it would be like speaking into a speaker with the power off.

Another way, of course, is to throw up the etheric screen, as we mentioned in a previous chapter. Also, one could focus in the now moment and think consciously that what he was saying has no impact upon you. The only thought that you would care to receive would be of positive growing influence and anything else would not be needed. This is to say that you only need experience from the highest source. That's what the master would do.

Now, let us say you meet someone and you immediately do not like his looks. The thought would come to mind, "I don't like you." Already, you are in trouble, for you would be giving this being artificial power over you by entering the state of fear. When you are conscious of this happening, I would strongly suggest immediately countering your image by, first of all, knowing that they have a God state. Secondly, try to remember that your ego does not know everything and it is basing its judgment from some past experience that is not valid here. Next, try to find something good or pleasant about the being in question. Stay in the now moment. Closely listen to what they are saying on all levels, not to what you are thinking. This is so important, for it would remove so much negativity from your life that you would more quickly, most quickly, evolve to a higher state of being. This would serve to keep you awake. This also would keep you aware of the various triggers that you would carry which would send you off to a different state of being or non-awareness.

You might say, "Sam makes me angry." Your masterful self would say, "I detect a feeling of anger about Sam. I think I will observe this and see whence it came." The false self would already be into it, reacting, whereby the masterful self would disconnect the ego and see if it could observe what label the false self was putting on Sam. Knowing what you do, the labels that you would put on Sam would cause Sam to react in a certain way, also.

There are times that you would go someplace and have a predetermined state of mind. Every time I drive down this street, I don't feel very well, so therefore, I know I won't feel very well if I drive down this street. It would be interesting to find out that the next time you drove down this street, you would stop yourself prior to the visit and say, "This is an entirely new event that has never happened before and let me see if this time, I can pick up a different feeling from driving down this street. I will endeavor to find something different on this street this time that I never saw before. I will observe a tree or a house that is pleasing to me and record that in my sphere, to be used in the event that I ever drive down this street again." Now, what have we done here?

*"You showed us a way to change our thoughts which would change our moods, which is wonderful."*

(Amazingly, Johnny comes in and proceeds to tell us how he has reprogrammed his thinking about washing the dishes. In the past, he looked at it as an unpleasant chore. He now sees it as doing something nice to help out.)

The important thing here is to stay in the now moment by removing the past by reprogramming conscious thought constantly with new information which, in effect, keeps you in the now state.

You have learned something after our brief respite from working on this book that will be of tremendous value to you. Certain meanings are attached to certain words and as long as the meanings that you attach to them coincide with what the world attaches to them, communication of thought goes on unhampered. What beings do not realize or tend to forget is that other beings think differently about the meaning attached to a word than they do. Why don't we use the example that has caused you much difficulty over some time? Now, let us take your favorite word and see how this could be misconstrued into sometimes distressing difficulty. What is your favorite word now?

*"Nice. Yuk!"*

Now, what did this word mean to you?

*"Phony."*

Now, why would this mean phony?

*"I associated the word 'nice' with someone being phony to get something he wanted."*

Now, the dictionary describes "nice" as pleasing, well mannered, as a nice child, or, that is nice music. Where do you think the meaning came from that you attached to it?

*"From being around people who, when they wanted something, would act pleasing, well mannered, ingratiating."*

Many beings would regard the word as having a pleasing connotation. This is just like, as you are well aware, our fabled conversation with George, who in conversation with you, would take the opposite meaning from what was meant and carry on a separate conversation with you at the same time you would carry on a separate conversation with him and neither one would be speaking on the same subject. This is a very difficult area for beings. The reason this is so difficult is that no one would have exactly the same meaning attached to the same word or words. It was an interesting discovery to all when you and John spoke to another couple and they, in turn, had different meanings yet to the word "nice." From just this one word, then, if that were the only word that beings would use, much confusion would result. Now, I am opening up a new area for concern here, for each word then could act as a trigger to bring out a myriad of confusion in communication. We could say, "nice being." That would have a meaning attached by every being who would hear it. Now, I make a point of this because of its importance.

Describe the typical nice being to you, a caricature.

*"Someone who is overdoing the complimentary, gracious, generous behavior and you know he wants something or he wouldn't be doing all this, but you don't know what he wants. It drives me crazy."*

All right. What I was trying to get you to describe was a particular look to someone, but that is not your identification. John would view a nice person as one who would radiate a pleasing frequency of energy whereby other beings would like to be around him because they like him. Generally, those radiating such energy would be regarded as likeable. How does this strike you?

*"I would like that kind of a person, too; too much to call him 'nice.' I would describe him as genuine or truthful or real."*

Factual?

*"Believable."*

What's the difference between factual and believable?

*"I want to use my own word. There's a difference to me."*

You can see plainly, factually, how conversation cannot be quite believable.

*"That was good, excellent. I would not want to face you in a debate!"*

Your dear friend would then say, "You are engaging in an exercise of semantics. One way this is true; in the other, it is not."

What does the word "evasive" mean to you?

*"Not honest."*

The dictionary, again, would say "elusive and not frank" (and certainly not Paul or John). Is this a nice word to you?

*"No, it has other meanings, also, like sneaky."*

Now, you have associated the word "nice" in its correct sense with the word "evasive." By its correct sense, I mean its dictionary definition.

What would the word "postpone" mean to you? Is it a nice word?

*"It means putting off something you don't want to do. It's not nice or unnice. It's a way out."*

What if a tennis match was postponed by rain?

*"Then I would figure one of the tennis players didn't want to show up."*

I like that and it certainly is a good way of yours to evade the issue, a nice way. I have selected some words, knowing you, that would necessarily have a different meaning to you than that taken from a dictionary. I only cite the dictionary as a source for common meaning.

I have started something here by showing that the words that you or any being would distort to suit your purpose would be negative triggers in response to your particular behavior patterns.

Each word that, by some accident, one would discover had its attached meaning different from common meaning or dictionary meaning, would be a word that one could analyze and track down the source of much difficulty of stress in one's life. This is different than the association I was discussing earlier. These are attached meanings to symbols. If they have common root, then correct or good communication would result. If the meanings are different, wars could start. How long did you and John go on prior to the discovery of the difference in meaning that you attached to these words?

*"A year and a half."*

It is fortunate, as you would expect, that there is a solution to this kind of dilemma. Let us say that one would discover a difference in communication or a problem in communication causing stress. One can start throwing out words, surrounding or in association with the problem area. When the field of words is narrowed down to a few, such as the few I chose for you, then the common definition and your definition can be compared and assessed. After assessment, then a synonym can be impressed into the sphere. Here is a method by which this can be worked out.

Take the word "nice," for instance. Write it on a piece of paper and next to it, write the meaning "genuine." Now, in your case, this would be a replacement word for the word that causes trouble. Then you could write on the same piece of paper, below it, "John is not a nice person, but a genuine person." You have then disassociated John or anyone else from the negative influence of the word "nice." So, every time you hear, "John is a nice person," substitute the word "genuine" in your mind until the two mesh or coincide.

John had a word, also, that had a very negative connotation to him and that would be the word "defensive." Unfortunately for you, you did not know this and you used it every so often with good intentions. Now, he is substituting the word "threatened" for "defensive" and he may live happily ever after, also.

As an interesting sidelight to this, unknown to you was that the word "nice" built up to the place that it had become so reprehensible to you that it actually caused a severe pain in your shoulder. This only came out and the pain was alleviated after much searching by you for the cause of this pain. Physical pain can result from the overuse or misuse of an understanding of a particular word.

Let us say that a couple you would know were having a difficult time with their communication with each other. With their permission, you could then ask each of them to describe a word or words which would bring out the offensive emotional feeling. You could then, in the same way, help them to reprogram their association, to disassociate the attendant feeling or charge from their sphere in regard to the other partner. This seems so simple in its concept that at first it would appear that it is too simple to work. Is that not correct?

*"It would appear that way, but I know what I've been through to overcome it."*

In its very simplicity, then, the truth would be presented. Beings would take a word that would be charged in some fashion, pile distorted meaning to it and then attach the meaning to another being and then react each time the word would come up without knowing whence it came. Now, guess where this leads to next?

*"I'm afraid to guess!"*

Actions or gestures. If one finds himself becoming annoyed with a gesture or habit of another, this is a signal that with this gesture or habit, there are certain thoughts that are put out that are particularly distasteful to one. If the thought that was put out with the offensive gesture or habit could be transduced or neutralized, then the offending action would no longer be offensive, would it? Certainly, all beings have habits that cause reactions within others. I'm not speaking of those which are threatening, but of those that would seem innocuous. The annoyance that is conveyed would project a particular way of thinking, not the action in and of itself. For instance, if one were in a love state, then it would be difficult to find an offensive action. If one were feeling poorly of himself or had low self-esteem, then many actions of others may become offensive. The focus would then be on the external not the internal. Know then that if one is triggered by an offensive action, that somehow one has gotten off the track and would be thinking poorly of himself.

One of the more common, hidden thoughts that need be

neutralized would be the one which states, "I don't deserve this." Many beings would attach this to any thought of improving themselves or raising their vibrations. Another way to paraphrase this is, "This is too good to be true." If either of these thoughts come up and it becomes a common habit of thinkng, then one can readily neutralize it by asking which "I" is speaking. Know then when this type of thought is produced, it is of necessity lower thought and need be countered immediately with, "Who says so!" We then speak of counter thought here. If a brush fire is burning, light a backfire to control it. For each negative thought, then, that is engendered, a counter thought need be imposed or attached to it to neutralize it.

It is becoming aware of your thought in the now moment that is important for you to be able to neutralize the negative ones. Let us try an exercise.

Now, for thirty seconds, I had you focus on an object of your choice. You chose a button, correct?

*"Yes."*

In that thirty seconds, you counted eight thoughts. Now, admittedly, with this focus, it probably slowed down the thought process. To my dismay, if a being would average sixteen waking hours per day, then with sixteen thoughts per minute, it would generate over fifteen thousand thoughts that would be readily discernible to the conscious mind if you were aware. Of these thoughts, some would be positive, some would be neutral and some would be negative. Your mission, then, would be to discern the negative ones and if they would be destructive to you, to neutralize them. If you would practice becoming aware of negative thoughts and countering them, in but a few days, the process would be nearly automatic. But, oh, the benefits that would accrue, for in no time, you would change the direction of your being to one of happiness.

# CHAPTER 9

## REDIRECTING THOUGHT

When beings find themselves feeling low or in a negative frame of mind, generally there has been an influence from the subconscious or taken in from the external, casting a pall over their otherwise naturally cheerful outlook. This tends to be a mystery to beings because the influence seemingly slips in undetected. Now, you had two telephone conversations today. One was positive, one was negative. Correct?

*"Correct."*

How did the positive one leave you?

*"It left me feeling cheerful."*

How did the other one leave you?

*"I felt tired."*

So, the influence of the moods of the two other beings was quite dramatic.

*"Yes."*

When I was fooling around with the disconnected telephone, I was showing you how to redirect thought. The conversation might go like this: "Hello, Thought. I see you are negative today and I am sorry, for I am not. Please go on with what you have to say and I will politely listen for a while, but since you are not of right mind, the words you say will have no influence upon me."

Naturally, you are not saying this in the verbal sense, but are thinking it, pulling the plug on the negative influence and only listening to words with no emotional charge. Realize then, that what the negative being is saying could be but turned around in an hour or a day or so and the same thoughts could be given to you with a happy charge placed upon them. It is the same person, but he is influenced, then, by a positive emotional charge. You can consciously let in the energy of those who are bright and cheerful and it will add to yours, making for synergy, boosting the vibration of both.

Another way of looking at the negative influence is viewing it as someone attempting to make you feel as bad as he does, so that you both would be equally miserable. What is the point to this? Why listen to him? Why would you listen to him?

*"Because we're friends and I owe it to him."*

That is an excellent comment because many beings do exactly this without realizing it. They would literally give up their higher vibrations to be on the lower vibrations of their friends, when they are in them. One does this in the guise of helping another with a sympathetic ear, but what have you really done? You have decreased your own vibrations without helping them at all.

Let us take another approach. Why not send them a spiral of white energy, as your dear friend suggested, and listen to every other word? Do you know what this would do?

*"It would disconnect me from the negativity."*

Do you know why?

(Silence.)

Gotcha! (Seth is exceptionally cheerful today.) By listening to every other word, which takes a bit of effort, initially, it has the effect of breaking their thought chain. Another way of looking at it is that you only receive one-half the energy that is sent by them. Let us demonstrate. "Hi, ~~I~~ am ~~negative~~ thought. ~~I~~ am ~~feeling~~ terrible ~~today~~." If you use this technique, then you would disconnect the connecting variable so that only random energy would be implanted in your sphere, resulting in no complete thoughts or connections, thus erasing the negative influence. Do you think that this would work for you?

*"I think with a little practice, it would work very well. It certainly is worth a try."*

It is not to be construed that one would not have empathy for the plight of others, but only to keep your vibrations at a higher level so that you can help them. It is important with this technique, to remain in the now moment or conscious of what you are being. What you are doing, in effect, is allowing or choosing the influence that you desire to receive. Although it may seem ridiculous, one could practice this technique, as I showed you, by using a disconnected telephone to program your thoughts when the real thing happens. Pick up the telephone receiver and have a simulated conversation.

Another way of accomplishing the same would be to have the conversation as a string of words that would be just flowing over the top of your head. There is psychological reason or trick for this. One other way to get around the negativity is when you first hear or feel the negative vibration, suddenly start talking of a positive experience that you have had recently and expound on that. This can have a magical effect and would benefit both of you, for what the negative being is saying is not what is really going on.

There are many negative influences that would strike you each day, both from within and without. If one would see a negative headline in a newspaper and would start to identify, such as, "Isn't that terrible?" then it would behoove one to find another word or phrase that would be of a positive note and would leave the so-called lasting impression. You have then redirected the negative energy. The first problem, of course, is to become attuned or aware of anything negative. Why would you need it? You would regard this, then, as a negative thought track. The ego identifies with calamity, terror and many other forms of negativity. It tries to make itself better by seeing the misfortune of another, but only succeeds in dragging in the negativity with this mode of operation. Can you name something that would influence you to feel negative?

*"Depressing movies can leave me feeling sad for awhile."*

Why would you go to them?

*"There's some kind of a morbid curiosity or attraction to them."*

If I would ask you how you would like to feel all of the time, what would you say?

*"I'd like to feel happy all of the time."*

This is consistent with most beings, for they would answer the same way. But there is something amiss here, for I have noticed that there is tremendous interest in negative stories in books, newspapers and films. If there would be no interest in feeling depressed, then the market for this negativity would not exist. Isn't that so?

*"There's truth in this, because sometimes I am really drawn to these stories and I will retell these stories to my friends so that we can all be properly shocked."*

Do you know what an allergy is?

*"I know I have some."*

Can you name one?

*"I'm allergic to sugar."*

Do you ever eat cookies?

*"Sometimes."*

How does this make you feel?

*"It makes me feel tired and in a bad mood."*

Isn't that strange?

*"Yes, because I know before I eat them that I will feel bad and then I will want more."*

Now, looking at this, this would be insane, as you implied. Obviously, this is a compulsion that would come directly from the false self. Now, this is the same way that you felt when your negative friend was being negative in the telephone conversation. Isn't that true?

*"Yes."*

Then this is insane, also. I don't mean to single you out, but I am using you as an example for most beings. What I am saying here is that most beings have allergies and *negative thought is just another allergy.* How does that strike you?

*"It killed my desire for cookies."*

Now, unbeknownst to you, you have two friends who do not view thought in this context; one, all of the time and one, part of the time. What would happen with the first is that he has gotten far enough with redirecting thought that he would view the watching of a negative film or any other negative thought as having a direct causal connection to depression, tiredness and disease. If you would give him a choice between a number of movies, which one will he always pick?

*"The happy ones."*

Always. Why is that?

*"Because he likes being happy."*

So, what you are saying, then, truthfully, is that you like being unhappy.

*"I guess I crave it sometimes, like cookies, even though I know in advance it will have a negative effect on me."*

Would you know how to stop this?

*"Being aware of it gives me the choice."*

Maybe there need be a pill on the market that would alleviate suffering from this allergy. What do you think?

*"I wonder if people would take it."*

I wonder, also. But in case they wouldn't, since it doesn't exist anyway, I have another idea. Before choosing to do anything, one could picture two large rectangles on the wall. They would be approximately four inches high and about fourteen inches long. One could be placed exactly next to the other. Within the first one, in the center would be a large 1 and in the second would be a large 2. The first one would be bright white in color and the second would be solid black. The first one would be associated with cause and the second one with effect. Now, let us say you are selecting a film. Before choosing the film, picture the two rectangles. Can you do this?

*"Yes. I chose not to see the film."*

Now, you assumed, automatically, I was speaking of a negative film, but I didn't say this. Automatically, you and most beings would take this posture. Now, you can see what takes place. This technique will work in all cases of negative thought. All one need do is just picture this and the resulting cause will give you a choice, not automatic rote behavior. In most cases, this will alleviate the allergic behavior to negative thought. If you can just be aware of where you are prior to making a choice, then the automatic programming into allergic negativity will be averted. In other words, a trick to stay into the now moment.

(A few days later, Seth pops in with a number of pieces of copper.)

Hello. How did the experimenting go with the white and black device?

*"It really works!"*

It worked so well that you even told your friends about it. What specifically did you find that it did?

*"I thought about eating a few cookies at lunch yesterday. A picture of the two rectangles came into my mind and I decided it wasn't worth it and did not eat the cookies. That's just one example. I've used the technique for many decisions during the few days since I learned about it and it's saved me a lot of trouble."*

The idea behind this, then, was to use thought to redirect thought so that you would not be controlled by addiction, just choice.

Now, let us assume that for some reason, addictive thought comes in and would have taken control. Then the mood is entrenched and you are once again caught in the clutches of a bad mood or negative thought. For example, you find yourself watching a very negative movie. Now being somewhat aware of cause and effect from the black and white rectangles, a thought may hit you. How do I get out of this addiction so I won't feel bad? Whenever a particularly dramatic, depressing scene is displayed and you are surprised, take the energy from the scene and send it to the north of you. Have it go in the direction of the North Pole, to the frozen reaches where it is impounded in ice in perpetuity. Can you do this?

*"I'm sure I can."*

Another way of disposing of this excess negativity when caught in it is to imagine it barely skimming your consciousness. Your consciousness would look like a large, white globe and it barely touches the surface and is repelled. This has the effect of you observing the negativity but not allowing it in. What do you think of that?

*"That would be easy."*

Now, if it has slipped by you and it is already entrenched, it probably would have a fresh trail into your sphere. You could literally reach into your sphere with your hand and pull it back out, symbolically, and throw it away.

Let us say, then, that one of these negative thoughts is pretty well entrenched and you know something is there, but you don't know where it came from or what it is. Have a friend, who would not think that you were off balance if you suggested it, hold up a piece of copper, crystal or his finger and point it at your sphere. Both concentrate on stirring up the negative thought so that it will boil up to the surface so that you will know what it is. Once you have surfaced it, then the solution is to send it away. By sending it away, then you would allow the universe to come in and heal the wound. Did you know you might have a wounded sphere?

*"No, I didn't know that."*

Now, there would be a question for those who face depression of how to transfer or redirect this negative thought into a more positive area of the sphere. Since the fear has positive and negative charges within it, one need redirect one's focus from the negative part of the sphere to the more positive or higher aspect of it. Now, so far I have described a sphere as a collection of thought with many aspects to it and you would imagine it like a round bowl of water. Is that not true?

*"That's how I see it."*

All things in the universe are spirals. There is no exception to the sphere. As you would go from the lower, heavier thought and start winding upward, then each turn around your sphere would be higher and higher in vibration. There are nearly infinite focuses along a being's sphere. Where you rest, at a given time, would be of the person that you are at that given time, speaking and thinking. Seldom do you rest at the same focus twice. In fact, never would you focus from the same vibration twice. Your focus at any given time would be from what total charge would be in charge at that particular time. That is, the influence of all of the charged thought energy that would be focused within you at a given time would equal your personality at that time. If all of the charges totalled together would be balanced on a higher level of your sphere, then your charge would be from love and would be toward the brighter side of the color spectrum. If most of the charge were coming from the lower part of the spiral, then your balance would be on the negative side and your vibration would be of a heavier, somber mood. The sphere could be unbalanced, then, from the right or to the left. Guess which is which? If the sphere is tilted downward to the left of the being, then the preponderance of negative charge is below the vibration of the particular being. If it is tilted to the right, then the positive, happy charge becomes as ecstacy or higher than the vibration of the particular being. The reader need not worry if you haven't seen a sphere, as it is a descriptive term. But as evolution continues, their appearance will come into your seeing.

Consciousness, or the sphere, as we have seen, has many protective mechanisms within it that would prevent, without the soul's permission, the release of a charged thought that would provide such high energy that it would overwhelm most beings. That is to say, if something would be too great a shock, as electrical energy, that would throw a being too far out of balance, then the protective mechanisms within the sphere, under most conditions, would block its uncovering.

As you have seen from readings performed, with the permission of several beings, it only takes a matter of minutes sometimes, using these techniques to unlock the door to problems that have run their lives, sometimes for nearly their whole lives.

With the mastery of these techniques, beings could then search out and release their heavy energy, making their lives brighter and happier and more attuned to greater awareness. There is another little experiment that I would share with you.

Now, we have wound a piece of copper wire in a spherical fashion with about seven turns in an upward, counterclockwise direction. We take two metal clips and clip the one in your right hand to the top of the wire and the left one at various intervals from the bottom of the wire upward to the top. This had the effect of refocusing your thought in a manner that would reflect a level of charge in your sphere, depending on where it is intersected. So, initially, when you did this, what happened?

*"When I picked up the wires, I felt nothing in my right hand. I felt an electrical charge in my left hand, so I clipped the left wire to a higher spot on the spiral until both hands felt the same."*

Then the place and time that you felt both hands as equal represented your particular state of your sphere or focus in the now moment. So, in effect, what we have done here is transduce the electrical energy of your sphere into the spiral by you holding it. Now, beings have much difficulty with their allergic state of mind when they become fixed to a certain outcome such as guilt or anger and have a difficult time getting out of this negative groove. If one then is tired of the state of your sphere, then one can use this spiral to energize another focus in the sphere.

(We then try another experiment.)

So changing the wires and letting your body energy stabilize causes the sphere to focus on a different level. As you keep changing the left hand wire or clip, you would then tend to focus on another level once it has stabilized. This may take a minute or two for stability.

Many have tried drugs and alcohol to control their moods, but the long term effect is only detrimental. By practicing changing the natural energy flow of your sphere by this method and some others I will discuss, then becoming attuned to adjusting your energy becomes easier. It is important to realize that when you change your focus, you do not attempt to bury or cover over that which need be looked at which would be the problem that created the negative focus to begin with. The idea is only to focus from another level than where the problem exists rather than to focus from the level of the problem.

When looking at a problem from a different focus with different energy, then the solution hanging in and around the problem becomes more readily ascertainable. This is why many would walk away from a problem and not think of it, to give the greater mind time to focus in on the problem.

When one would focus on a problem, the ego would then, on many occasions, cover over the cause or solution to the problem. We have seen this on many occasions. Using word association, one would begin to look at a problem only to find that it leads somewhere else, then somewhere again and where one wound up at the root or solution of the problem, one never would have imagined from the beginning that it would be attached in this manner. The ego is very adept at burying problems in its graveyard. Out of sight, out of mind.

One of the larger problems, then, is in finding solutions that generate negative energy from problems stemming from the dream state. Now, this could be the sleeping, conscious state or the awake, conscious state of dreams. Let us try something else.

If I say "dream," what do you say?

"*Reveal.*"

"Space."

"*Time.*"

"Event."

"*Blank.*"

"Block."

"*Remove.*"

"What, Blue."

"*Ocean.*"

Now, what we have done here is attempt to pull out that which would go on in the awake dream state. If one would find what is being worked on in this state at a given time and become aware of it, then one could speed the process by consciously going with it. Now, our first attempt was not altogether succussful, was it? What do you think it was that interferred with it?

"*My state of mind at the time. I was very scattered that day.*"

Are you scattered now?

"*No, I'm clear now.*"

All right, we have just tried it again. Not wishing to bore the reader with the details, we'll leave out the words used for the associations. But with a clear mind, that is, a focused mind, was the result achieved?

"*Yes, it was. I became aware of a dream that was going on underneath the surface which would have an effect on my mood.*"

You then found that you were working out your feelings about current weather conditions.

"*Yes, it's been raining here for two weeks. I was dreaming of a bright, sunny, summer day.*"

Now, let us say that underneath the surface, you were working out something that I was trying to bring out of you the last time, delusion. The reason you were so scattered was that you were working out, underneath the surface, a way around the delusion of what you were feeling and the non-action you were taking. Now, it begins to make sense, doesn't it?

"*Yes.*"

Many times, then, there would be a feeling of being lost or scattered and the thought behind it is elusive. If this would happen, one could then postpone attempting to pull out the reason for the confusion for about an hour and then try again. Two things would happen. One, the dream would be finished or worked out, or two, there would be sufficient change to enable one to arrive at the conclusion.

Let us say, then, you are able to pull out what is being worked on in this state. If you do not like the feeling or the direction it is taking, then you would take this and, closing the eyes and taking a few deep breaths, redirect the mind or sphere to another solution. As yet, you do not have the power, by yourself, to change the weather. So, you could redirect the thought energy to something of greater interest. What is another interest of yours?

*"Traveling."*

You could then focus on a location for a trip that you would like to take. In the closed-eye state, direct your sphere to come up with a solution to any obstacles standing in the way of taking this trip to your selected location. So, we can pull out a state and find out what it is, then redirect it to something more useful or practical. Why waste inner resources? This was an example of something being worked out that was of little practical value and could be redirected to something more useful.

Now, let us say that you had some pain, physical or mental. You could then direct your sphere to work out a solution to the pain. You could instruct it to work out this pain in the awake or asleep state, continuing with the process until it arrived at an acceptable solution. Yes, that is right. You can use your inner resources in the dream state one hundred percent of the time. You needn't limit it to your sleeping hours.

We have discused using thought to manifest objects. Let us say, then, that you have put forth a white thought, asking the universe to provide something. Your desire arrives, but let us say, something has gone wrong and the object you wished is not shiny and new, but old and dilapidated. Somehow, somewhere, your thought was misdirected. Then all you need do is let go of it when this is realized and redirect a white thought to the universe, having it bring this into fruition within a designated time which you would deem as reasonable. So, in effect, you would be re-accessing the universe toward manifesting your desire.

When negative thoughts come into you, with a little practice, you would, in effect, catch them and send them back out to re-energize into something that would be more useful. If one had thoughts that a current weather pattern would go on and on and start to drag him down, then one would redirect his thinking. One of the ways that this could be accomplished, of course, is to focus on a gold light or gold object. This particular influence would have the effect of bringing in another energy that would refocus the conscious attention to a higher level which would automatically bring in other subjects of interest.

If you find yourself around a group of people and the discussion has taken on an aspect of negativity not to your liking, then there are ways of redirecting the energy of the group in a way that will lift the spirits of all. The discussion might be one of a current disaster, such as a flood or airplane crash. When it is your turn to communicate your feelings on the subject, it is but a simple matter to direct your part of the conversation to another level by bringing in a fact such as how safe airplane travel is versus driving a car. If it is a discussion of a flood, ask a question of the group of how long it has been since a flood had struck that particular area. What have you done here? You have opened up to the thought of others the possibility that these are remote incidents and as a general fact, they are rare, indeed. What you have done here is bring in the probability of a more positive approach to a conversation, redirecting the energy of the group to a higher level of thought energy, raising the vibrations of the group. As you have seen, each group of beings will have a merged energy or synergy. If the synergy takes on a lower vibrational mood, then all will be affected in a negative manner. Now, you have this friend who is quite adept at spotting this and would start out with the most negative member of the group, whetting his interest, raising his vibration and proceedintg to then lift the vibrations of the group by using humor and getting them all involved. In no time, the group becomes animated and raises its vibrations as a whole. Have you ever encountered a situation like this?

*"Yes, I have, more than once. I have been in rooms filled with people who were feeling negative and I, being in a good mood, felt out of place."*

You were in place. That is to say, if you refuse to let yourself feel negative in a group, it will not be long before the group will begin to respond. In other words, do not let yourself listen to negativity. It almost goes without saying, do not act superior, either. When the opportunity arises, then, let your state of energy flow.

*"This brings up a question. When I have walked into some groups, I felt that I was being judged. In some instances, it made*

*me feel insecure. In others, I felt that I was picking up the judg-
ment of the group and I didn't like it. It made me feel uncomfortable. In these situations, I made a conscious decision that I had
nothing to prove. I know what I know and I am who I am and
others can take it or leave it, but I've worked too hard to com-
promise being true to myself."*

I like the technique that John uses in these situations. When he
feels like this, he then will program an expanse of time, be it five
minutes or longer, where he will do nothing and wait for the
result. He won't be friendly or unfriendly, but will just be, until
the new synergy of the group with his added energy, stabilizes.

*"Well, that's one of the reasons I keep him around."*

There is something else that can be generated, also, in raising
the vibrations of a group. You can consciously send energy with
your thought of love to the group and it will be heard at some
level. Someone might wish to argue with this as being simplistic
and invalid, but in light of what has been discussed so far, this is
a much happier alternative.

There is one other idea that may help if you would find yourself
in dark thought. Consciously image a bright light that you would
be able to turn on by throwing a switch. This light is always with
you and all you need do is turn it on. Try it.

*"Okay."*

What happened?

*"Well, I've stopped yawning, haven't I?"*

Yes, it has the effect of energizing you when, for reasons that
you are unaware of, you are in a particular state and desire a
change.

If a couple has gotten into a situation whereby a particular
habit of one would constantly irritate the other and nothing was
changing, then the only change in direction would be in redirecting the energy of the thought behind it. Confront the fear and
what will result will have a very interesting effect, one that will
surprise you.

An example of this is the one that you brought up, concerning
John's bad habit, according to you, of clipping his beard.

*"Yes, every morning he clips his beard and leaves little
whiskers lying all over the bathroom sink. For a long time, I
didn't say anything. When it finally became unbearable, the*

*resentment, that is, I told him I didn't like it."*

What happened?

*"He replied quite directly, but in a friendly manner, that this was a condition of the marriage and that I had agreed to accept it."*

His response was so different from what you expected that it changed your attitude about the offensive habit, didn't it?

*"Yes, it did. It was so funny that it no longer bothers me."*

(Seth takes out a large scissors and proceeds to cut little whiskers out of John's beard.)

Each couple would then have certain habits that would affect the other partner. But if a non-defensive, humorous response is given in confrontation, the energy is then redirected and the problem is surfaced and removed.

The reader will probably use the examples that I have given as a springboard to many other interesting ways of redirecting thought.

# CHAPTER 10

## CONTROL OF THOUGHT

The word "control" in the spirit of this book would imply *being aware* of thought to be in control.

To take control would also be "out of control" in certain aspects of thought transmission.

First, let us now, in detail, describe word association in such a way that all who choose to use it may understand it. Certain words then are keys to bring out certain thought change, for example "dream." Using this word then unlocks the particular thought group that is associated with dreams. If I were reading you and I used the word "dream" then you would follow, as you have, with "night." Following this, I would then associate a color, such as "blue" and you would probably say something like "sky." Now, so far we have unlocked two separate chains of thought to probe into the sphere to this level. The next word would be something like "key" or "time" or event." If this is followed by you with a word after each word I would say, then we are progressing into the sphere to find the storage bank of thoughts that we are looking for. For the purpose of this illustration, we would be looking for your most recent dream or a current dream. So of course, you would use somewhere in your list of words the word "current." Followed by this, you could say "time of day" and then "picture." At this level, if a feeling or picture or words come to mind, you would then begin relating that certain portion of thought associated with these words and begin to explain it with the resulting feeling and colorations plus emotional charge. Sometimes, then, dreams would need interpretation, but the key to them would be the feelings that would go along with them. For instance, if the feelings were depressing or dark, then they might be associated with some kind of guilt. If they were bright and cheerful, you might be working out some sort of current interrelationship in your life. If the feeling is hidden, then something has taken place that is beyond your conscious grasp or, in other words, something that you have not worked out. You may then go on using the word "deeper" with a response and then the word "underlying" with a response and then the question from that new level. Each time something is hidden, you can use the word "deeper" and the word "underlying" and then the word "picture" to present what is available on that level of understanding.

It isn't clear at times what it is that would ride underneath the stored thought. At times, the stored thought would have such an emotional charge that its release would overwhelm you and send you into a chain reaction of such energy that it would be too destructive for you to handle. Has this ever happened to you?

*"Once it nearly happened."*

Yes, but the overload of charge was such that it was dispersed over three or four days. At that particular time, though, it was I who ignited the release of this particular charge, using a copper rod with energy to bring this out. It would not have been released normally with the normal word association that I am teaching.

Now, dreams are just one area that would have clues to bring to the surface what may be influencing you at a given time. Almost all beings have hidden reservoirs of thought influencing them, as we have seen in previous chapters. As we have also seen, that which seems to be causing a difficulty may be entirely different from that which first meets the eye. For instance, you may think you might have a sexual problem and it may turn out to be some sort of anger that started when you were but a child.

Another area that is of interest is then to go back and somehow find, in a short period of time, the event or events that would be generating an irrational mode of behavior. Let us take anger, for instance. You would start with the word "problem" or "anger" and then use a color such as "red." After each response, you would then follow it with another word probably to at least six different words to arrive at the proposed level of the problem. Initially, this would take some practice to get to the level where the energetic particle of thought is stored in your sphere. Now, in the experiments with other beings that you have witnessed, how long would it generally take to get to the average problem?

*"Ten to thirty minutes."*

Now, admittedly I have a little advantage in being able to read these problems in beings' spheres. But, with a little practice, all beings then can take any problem and go through a list of words centered around that problem, ending with the words "underlying" and "picture," and at least some portion of the difficulty will be pulled out for them to see.

One of the difficulties in using this technique has been that beings could not recognize the solution to the problem even when it was presented to them orally or in written form. The advantage to this technique is that it will bring out the stored difficulty in most cases as long as the energy is not too high, allowing beings to view it. Even if the solution is not recognized, at least bringing it to the surface can prevent it from spreading further. Having the solution, even though unrecognized, sitting there in front of their eyes, will eventually spark first their curiosity, then recognition.

Fear of the solution is what blocks most beings' attempts to overcome the problem. When the solution is presented, using this technique, then fear need be disconnected so the solution may be viewed in its true light. How does one disconnect fear?

*"Decide to stand back and observe it like it was happening to someone else."*

Excellent. Another way is to somehow bring in humor. Humor disconnects fear as fast as any other method of dealing with it. If all else fails, use a sense of humor. Have you ever noticed that if you are plodding along seriously, if someone strikes you with a funny joke, as John does occasionally, something outrageous, what happens to the fear?

*"It leaves."*

Yes. The ego or false self would try to make everything serious, but if it can somehow be viewed less seriously, humor seems to take the charge out of the emotion.

One of the cautions in using word association is that the result need not be feared. I wish to emphasize this strongly as the very fear itself will bring out blocking control variables to keep the solution hidden. If you are using this, by any means that you can come up with, reduce fear of the solution. You may start out one way, attempting to arrive at the deceit of your driving emotion. If the process becomes too heavy or serious, then throw in the words "funny" or "laugh" to disconnect the emotional charge. The idea, of course, is then to use word association to bring out that which is truly hidden to aid you in dismembering the hidden thought's emotional charge. You may have to use word association on a particular charged thought more than once, like weeding a garden, for sometimes the roots would remain. A technique you might use when you first bring out the offensive thought would be to mentally fill in the gaps with white light, which is, in effect, white thought.

If at any time, you just cannot get to a particular blocked thought, it only means that it would have such stored energy that its release would overwhelm you. If this be the case, then hit away at it a little at a time or keep chipping at the block until the energy is gradually released. Understand, then, that it might go somewhat slower for the unpracticed than for one such as I, who is thoroughly familiar with the technique. If at first you don't succeed, do not despair, for as I have indicated, this takes a little practice.

You will know when you have reached the solution when you as the subject feel the energy flow out of you or you are disconnected from the driving mechanism. Again, it should be emphasized that one would be in a relative degree of stability when using this method.

The primary motivator to avoid looking at problems would be that of fear. Fear then being the mother of all emotion, as is commonly known, need be disconnected with any sort of control of thought. One of the quickest ways to reduce fear is to write facts about it on a piece of paper. The false self, which is fear, absolutely abhors fact. The false self would be content to skate around any issue, worrying, making the fear larger than life by skipping over the facts. If any other type of emotion is a problem, such as jealousy, anger, guilt or the like, it would have, then, its common reduction to fear. If one of these emotions is a problem, put it down on paper and start listing facts until you end with fear. Then use facts to reduce the fear. If the fear would be one that would overwhelm you, then you need one of these other methods to reduce it until you can get control of it.

One of the first ways to control fear is to use or focus on a light blue color. It would be necessary to focus your full attention on this color for maybe up to ten minutes so that the emotion can be brought under control. It is fortunate that when the high charge of fear would strike you, it would be as any other allergy in that it would have its peaks and valleys. That is to say, it would not be at constant strength forever. If light blue is not available, then any pastel color other than yellow would still be assuaging to the high charge. If you would find that it would then be difficult to focus on a colored object, find a colored light and sit or lay under it. It will have the same effect, usually in about ten minutes. How does color affect your moods?

*"I use it a lot and it can change my moods. I use it along with certain tones."*

Which tones?

*"The chords of C and F are the most effective for me."*

Yes, we have a friend who would experiment with various sounds until a particular being would select one over another and then that would be the sound such as yours, which would resonate with his vibration in such a way as to calm him. Anyone can do this by going up and down the scale of an instrument until he finds the most pleasing sound to him. What effect, then, does this have on you?

*"I usually use it if I get very tired or depressed over something. It takes about ten minutes to remove the depression or tiredness. I often continue for longer periods because I enjoy the feeling."*

If, after one has selected a particular sound or chord and the feeling is one that is still offensive, then it would be better to select another one of like, pleasing quality and experiment with that one.

Many different colors of the lighter, brighter variety can then be experimented with to find the combination that would reduce offensive moods or to increase your energy to overcome it. The key here, and I can only emphasize it as strongly as words would permit, is to be *willing* to allow the change of the emotion. There are times when beings would then choose to soak up or stay in negative emotion for some period of time. They would choose to stay with it and savor it until it has run its course. Sometimes, the false self will have locked you in its negative tendrils in a way that would deceive you into being convinced that this is you. After some time, when you grow tired of it, it will then run its course and then you can turn the negative emotion on itself to engineer its own removal. After it has run its course, then you can determine that you do not want this offensive thought and then program your control variables in a way that you would tell them to turn this negative energy on itself. One of the ways that you can accomplish this is by agreeing, "All right, you are here, now. Give me all you have." Do you know what would happen then?

*"I think it would bring me out of it."*

Yes. Asking it to bring in more energy would then turn it on itself, bringing it under control. We are treating it as a separate object or one that would be separate from you. It is important to realize that it is not part of you, but a false creation that will disintegrate upon its realization as false. By doing this, you are bringing it into focus as being the nothing that it isn't. Do you understand this?

*"Yes, I do."*

Just to clarify a little further, take the fear and see what it is composed of. Look at it directly. See if it is what is actually there. I won't go into detail, but when you confronted one of your own fears, when you found what it was composed of, was it not different from what you thought?

*"Yes, it was."*

So, the fear then turned out to be something different than you would first imagine?

*"Yes."*

When one would start confronting fear, initially, the fear itself would try to run away with itself and hide, masquerading as something else. It is important to realize that the fear of anything is far worse than what is. Masters of self know that and then are capable of keeping their level of stress down and saving their energy in an efficient manner that would be foreign to most beings. It should be emphasized, then, that there is no fear in the now moment.

Two techniques that may seem quite esoteric come to mind which might be helpful to those wishing to get control in a particularly fearful situation. The first would be, take two quartz crystals, the larger the better, and place them each ten feet away from you, one on the right and one on the left. Sit on the floor or on a chair, the floor would be better, and concentrate, using your own thought power to increase your energy or raise your vibrations. It would be helpful to focus on or otherwise concentrate on pale orange as you would sit there with your eyes open or closed, if this works for you. What this does is to bring in energy to the edges of your sphere in a way that will lift you, with your willingness, above the lower energy problem and give you new sight on the fear. If one would choose to use such an experiment, one need have the openness and willingness to accept that this might work for him. If one would attempt this with judgment of results, then the effort would be meaningless.

*"I'm glad you're going into fear. I have so many friends who, for so many years have talked about the same problem in their lives, but seem unable to do anything but talk about it because of the fear of facing the problem."*

*"If I have a fear, one of two things will happen. If I'm consciously aware of what the fear is, I will be obsessed with it, talk constantly of it, think constantly of it. It will be the only thing I can think of. It paralyzes me, makes it impossible for me to get anything else worthwhile done. If I am not consciously aware of it, it still has the same result. I will be confused, distracted, unable to get anything done and then I add guilt to the fear because I'm not doing what I'm supposed to be doing. Then I get sick."*

*"Eventually, when the pain is great enough, it will drive me to go to the bookcase, get a spiritual book and start reading. Most spiritual books have something to say about fear. This will usually pull me out of the fear because it reminds me that whatever happens is only an obstacle that my soul has set up for me to overcome. By that time, the only important thing to me is to overcome the obstacle in the best way possible, which makes the fear melt away."*

There is no hierarchy among fear. That is to say, one fear would be no greater than another. It is just the energy or charge that one places with it that would make the seeming difference. As I have mentioned previously in this book, beings have a tendency toward engaging themselves in feeling bad or allergic thinking. If one finds himself on this chain of thought, one need do almost anything to sever the chain. Any diversion, once the emotional juggernaut of allergic thinking is engaged, would be helpful unless it has the aspects of procrastination. This tendency then need be reversed by facing the issue directly.

Another technique that might be used to disconnect fear would be to place two small bar magnets, one on each side of the head about one inch away and directly above the ear. What this will influence, of course, is to change your magnetic charge to a small degree which would elicit another focus which would view the fear from a different direction. Now, certainly no one would walk down the street holding upright two bar magnets or it might engender some strange feelings in others, who might believe you might be strange, indeed. Again, if no judgment is attached to the end result, the influence cannot but help change the direction of your thinking.

When one is engaged in emotionally charged fear thought, one could imagine a long wire attached to one's sphere, draining the excess energy slowly away into the ground. We are not speaking of lightning rods here, but only a flowing away of the excess, useless energy generated to solve the problem in need of a solution.

Do you know what fear is?

*"Any fear I've ever had, when I reduce it to the core, is caused by the thought that I cannot control the situation. It has never been anything but that. The problem is that when fear strikes, it is so overwhelming that I forget that and get involved in the emotion of the situation."*

There have been many books written about fear and dealing with it. Some of the most helpful have suggestions along the lines of "Think of God," "Pray to God," "Raise your Consciousness," until the feeling subsides. One of the problems then is one may have perfectly good intentions of doing just this, but the fear is so overwhelming that it would then appear real, more real than praying and asking for help. What is then necessary, assuming one is tired of fear, is to take it on and bring in greater amounts of fear. This has the opposite effect, for it then reduces the fear. Fear operates on fear, if you will. That is, fear operates on the avoidance of the solution or fear begets fear. Asking for more fear to come in then takes it on and in a strange way that would be difficult to explain, actually reduces its charge. Remember, the false self sees things backwards and when you turn it on itself by asking it to bring on more, it is incapable of doing so because it has already generated its maximum effort and by asking for more, it will actually turn it on itself. It actually would be playing its own game, to use fear to destroy fear. By calling the ego on its false generation, it would be, then, the facing of fear.

You have pointed out that two of the biggest fears facing friends of yours would be the fearing of the alienation of their loved ones' affection and the fear of financial failure. Now, let us say, then, that the ego would have you, as a being, suspicious of your loved one's loyalty. You might be imagining this or it might be fact. It matters not. Fear comes in, "What will I do?" Obviously, in this state, one feels forced to *do* something. The fear is then built up to an all-consuming attitude. It then takes over everything and would be the most important thing short of the disintegration of the planet. At this point, when one is caught up in such a hopeless state of affairs, one would switch gears and ask more fear to come in, more disloyalty, more alienation. Motion it with your hand. Signal it in. Ask it to compound itself. Give it all it has. Then when it has exhausted itself, try to think of a few situations that might even make it more disloyal and think of more places that the imagined, likely events will occur. Set the scene, so to speak. At this stage, the ego, with etheric holes shot through it, will generally realize it is beaten at its own game and it will decide to back off. Then, don't give up. Go after it. Chase it etherically down the street, so to speak. Beg it for more and you will find a strange thing happening. It becomes suspicious in its absence. You cannot find it and you'd wonder, where did it go? Have you ever tried this?

*"I believe I have and it got to the point that I really didn't care anymore."*

But the ego is forgetful, It would have you trying the same thing again and again, until eventually a groove is worn in your sphere and retraining, in effect, is in place.

Now, let's take another example. That would be fear of financial failure, wouldn't it? Ever had such a thing?

*"I sure have."*

What did you do about it?

*"Freaked out."*

What happened then, as you indicated, it continued to get worse until something changed. What was it that changed?

*"My attitude."*

Now, if one would be caught up in this, let us say the rent was due tomorrow and you had not the funds to cover it, then you might ask the ego, "This is not a great enough test. Why don't you bring in more? Why don't you come up with another place to live?" The ego then will say, "Tomorrow is Doomsday!" Notice that tomorrow never comes, because once tomorrow has arrived then the following day becomes Doomsday and on and on because that is the way of the ego. All you need do, then, is to call its bluff, for it holds no hand of cards.

There are, then, other parts of self that would help you in controlling the false self, which would be what I mean when I suggest controlling self. For, you certainly wouldn't wish to try to control the greater self, that which you would call intuition or something called the little voice. If you would then succeed in letting go of a particular fear thought and let the universe control it, the little voice will suddenly let you know a solution. The universe, through the little voice, with your false self out of the way, will flow solutions through to you until the message is taken in. In effect, this would be going with the flow.

Beings have groups of thought incorporating events or experience from the past that would proceed to solve new problems. This can then create many new, additional problems, It need be remembered that each now moment is unique unto itself and the exact now moment will never be repeated, never. Each new problem that comes up, even if it seems like an old one, will have a new solution that is not exactly like the old one. *It need be every reader's mission to remove the old solutions to new problems.* It should be remembered, then, that you will never run out of solutions. If something doesn't work, change it.

An interesting way to change your mood or way of thinking

would be to program thought by use of control variables and by programming your sphere to change color. Ever thought of that?

*"No, I can't say that I have."*

But you do it every day, don't you?"

*"How is that?"*

The selection of the colors you wear, for one. This would be a clue to where you're at. You automatically would allow some colors to influence you, unbeknownst to yourself, so your sphere, in effect, would color itself without you even knowing it. Wouldn't it be interesting if you woke up tomorrow morning and suddenly said, "Oh, I guess I'm in an orange mood today." Or, someone would call you on the phone and ask you, "How are you today?" And you would say, "Yellow, thank you." He might think you were cowardly or he might ask you what you were saying if he would be listening at all. Then you would say, "I think I will focus from a more energetic part of my sphere today." They might then say, "I'm blue today. I think I will be restful. What about Friday?" Obviously, this would seem a non-sensical conversation today, but with greater understanding, this would not be as remote as it would first seem. If you could then control your energy level by your thought, then you would take control of yourself, not sub-conscious, charged thought.

You might try an experiment and that would be to have a number of pieces of colored paper sitting by your bedside table. Every morning, pick up a different color and focus on it for a few seconds and see what influence in your mood and energy you would pick up in that day. Color has such influence in the lives of beings in the aspect of energy that it is little suspected. Look at the restful places that you would like, where you would spend leisure time. See what colors are available for you to look at there. Check the dominant colors, that is, the ones most prevalent. Bring the ones that are most restful into your life on more and more occasions. The difference in your life might surprise you. After finding your restful colors, then you can start programming them into your sphere. You would accomplish this by seeing or feeling the energy emanating from the colors and with closing your eyes for a few seconds, instill by imagination the color in your sphere or consciousness. It will have some positive effect upon you. While you are at it, if you would care to try it, try programming gold light. This will also have an interesting effect.

Beings have another ability and that would be of projecting thought or energy. Have you ever wondered why, when you thought of another being, it generally wasn't long before your paths would cross either by telephone or in person?

*"I have fun watching this work."*

Do you know how it works?

*"One or the other of us sends a message and we connect. But I usually don't know which one sends the message."*

This is a very interesting idea in that you are focused in the now moment and one would send simultaneous messages, which are energy. In effect, the thought would be a quick one and it would be timeless, which would require no time and space. If this is confusing, what I mean to say is the thoughts connect instananeously. So, if you think of your dear friends in San Francisco, then they are in turn thinking of you. If the thought is strong and persistent, then you will intersect them in the physical plane before long. Other forces then come into play which would bring this about.

Now, in my dimension, if I think of someone, he is instantly there. You may never have thought of this and I won't go far afield, but you can see then that in timelessness, thought just is and has no space to travel, bringing creation or transmission instantly to view. Think of the changes in your physical world if this would be the case. Now, I then mention this for some reason, don't I? Have you any idea what that is?

*"This time I have no idea."*

You also have this ability, but it would be limited by your thought. It would have to go in and out of time to be projected and would therefore have the limitations set upon it by the level from which it is projected.

*"So, both people are contacting each other?"*

Yes. But, either is limited by the degree to which he can receive the signal. Now, maybe you can see why like attracts like.

*"No."*

If your friends could not receive information from you at the level that they would dispense it to you, then they couldn't be your friends. If the friends were not on the same vibrational level as you, first of all, you would have little in common and secondly, you would have little to communicate. It would be as the example that we used earlier in the book where one being would be saying one thing and the other would be saying another and another. It would be as though you would speak a foreign language.

Ever notice that if you would change your occupation, how your friends would change?

*"It would be hard to miss that one."*

Yes, there is a certain bond of information that would be exchanged with those of like interests. If your interests then change, probably so would your occupation.

Now, since you would have like kind of interests and energy, it would not be so difficult to send information back and forth and to heal each other. Now, you have seen in the experiment with your dog that the feeling you project is quickly turned around and expressed by the dog. It is the same for beings. There might be a delay in the response but it would not go unnoticed on some level of communication.

Have you ever noticed how your animals know when you are home and when you aren't, even though you may be hidden from their sight or hearing?

*"Yes."*

How would they know this?

*"Their intuition."*

Now, beings then have the same thing, but it is not within the usual conscious knowing state. Let us say, then, that one would go into a store and would select an object for purchase and would have a choice of a number of beings who would collect for the object. If you were in this situation, would you use your intuition?

*"If you mean which clerk to go to, I'd definitely use my intuition."*

Do you know why you do this?

*"To make things as easy as possible on myself."*

You are one with a developed sense of intuition. All have it, but not all use it. You might select the same clerk at the same store every time and then all of a sudden decide to go to someone else, all things being equal. You might wonder why you did this and all of a sudden discover that there might be a lengthy delay by the one who you might normally have selected. This is an example of controlling your sphere in the now moment. Information is constantly being fed in that you could not put your consciousness in touch with. Assimilating it and using it in the now moment to your advantage would then save you much difficulty. This is the way of the universe where everything is already perfectly set in order. All you need do is follow it. It is the conscious interference with this natural flow by the ego which would send beings' lives on a rocky path.

The ego would want constant excitement which would then, in turn, interfere with this natural flow. The ego would seek, unknowingly, to manufacture trouble to keep itself supposedly in control and then would seek to render a solution where there was none to begin with. Do you see why it then would be regarded as the false self?

"*Yes.*"

Do not be afraid to rest "unknowingly in the bored state." When one would then get into this state, one then would be getting in touch with the greater, natural state where everything flows. There might be a period of restful "boredom" prior to the engaging of this higher state. You might regard this as a delay in time, but in effect, it is a saving in time. In this bored state, you could begin programming from this state your control variable, consciously, by asking that you would keep the conscious ego under control so that you could stand back and watch what is *really* happening. If you encounter problems in this state, think of them from the aspect of how would one who mastered the ego, that is, a God-self, solve this problem. Another way of looking at it is how would one "solution" this problem or water it down so that it would float to the surface with the rest of the residue.

We have already spoken of pulling in or pulling out negativity from within by use of many techniques including reaching in with your hand and pulling out the offending thought and cutting it off with a scissors and smashing it. Another way of accomplishing the same object but with a little more drama, is to write down what the offensive, driving thought mechanism entails in detail. Then take the piece of paper and burn it, watching it burn, or crumble it up and throw it in the trash. When you destroy the paper with these thoughts written on it, remember they are energy and that you have by this procedure or some variation of it, released them and let them go.

You have seen me accomplish this on more than one being, etherically, with equally gratifying results.

*"Yes, I have."*

Now, as we have learned, if you choose certain modes of behavior such as driving your automobile too fast or refusing to acknowledge the presence of other beings on the road, then the effect will be a traffic ticket or a wreck. Notice that I didn't say accident. As your dear friend would say, there are no accidents. When we mentioned this device which was white and black, illustrating cause and effect, if you then become conscious in the now moment, you would know that to choose certain methods of behavior will result in the same effect. What happens, however, is the groove in your sphere becomes increasingly charged and each resulting choice will build the charge into increasingly dramatic effects. It is like a trail that has become worn out and rutted. It will cause more and more damage as the choice becomes worn out. Remember it is not ever the same twice in spite of what the ego would dictate.

Some beings would choose certain irrational modes of behavior. They would elect to control the behavior of others by the use of anger, disapproval or withholding of approval or love and then would wonder why the world would be such a hostile environment. It is the old adage, if you are angry, so is the world. If you are in love, however, you will find the same state. Notice how stormy it becomes when you are stormy inside.

If beings would find that they leave behind them a trail of broken objects, somehow then, their behavior would suggest that they might be preoccupied or occupied by the ego, not the greater self. If one then has some sort of offensive behavior, then look to others for they will be your mirror, enabling you to then see it in yourself. If all of those around you would act confused, then you might know that something within you is confusing to them. It is so difficult at times for beings to see their own behavior. If then one would find that all of the beings around him would communicate poorly, then one might look at one's own brand of communication. I don't wish to focus on you directly, but so many beings fail to wake up and take note of their own thought and behavior resulting from it. It would seem that I'm going on and on about something that would be self-evident to everyone, but in essence, this area is overlooked by most. We are entering into a time of increased energy and a sleepy civilization is gradually awakening. Has this been a problem for you?

*"It's always been easier to notice other people's behavior more than my own."*

Now, in these times, then, you need pay increased attention to the behavior of others for it will change quite quickly. For reasons that would be obscure to you now, your behavior would come back to you more quickly than was evident previously, in time. It would be a time, then, of accelerated growth and those around you would form in concert. Watch, then, those who would seem to be expressing certain behavior around you and see if you can detect what it is that they are seeing in you.

Probably one of the strangest revelations that has come to you recently would be that of the apparent timelessness of the right side of the brain. Now, you would have a friend who is a friend to all of us, who would keep telling you, "Stay to the right, use the right path," or words to that effect. Now, you would have an explanation for this?

*"Yes, stay to the right means use the right side of your brain, the intuitive side."*

Yes. You can see, then, with the intersection of several different beings, that it inspired this revelation to you. What would happen, then, is the sphere or the timeless aspect of the sphere, would be connected to the right side of the brain or the timeless side and the logic side or the timed variety, more thoroughly known as conscious thought, would be connected to the left side or that in time. Now, the creative part of the brain or sphere connecting to it would be much more rapid and would be unlimited. The trick then would be learn to connect to the creative, greater aspect or timeless part of yourself.

Up until this point, in this book, I have led the readers through many new methods to learn to reprogram thought energy to allow them to enjoy a greater connection to their greater being. In attempting to describe how the lower function works in conjunction with the higher function, it would be necessary to understand how the lower function works so one could then reroute energy to the higher, swifter thought zone. Can you see, then, why it would be necessary to go through the lower thought zone to understand it thoroughly in order to tap into the higher zone?

*"I can understand why I had to do it, but with the increased energy now available, I'm wondering if others can understand without having to go through all that."*

It would depend, then, on what lessons it would be for their soul's growth. Did I answer that sufficiently?

*"Yes, I'll give you a B+ for that answer."*

That would be a timeless or a timed B+?

*"You would think I have learned not to try to upstage you by now, wouldn't you?"*

*(During the past several days, a series of amazing events involving meeting many people in various scientific fields took place, enabling John and me to understand the meaning of the last few paragraphs.)*

Yes, I am sure the universe arranges little demonstrations through other beings that would put a stamp of approval on learning new information.

*"That's the understatement of the solar system in our time frame!"*

Let me explain a little how this works. If one would be triggered into anger, getting into the lower self, that is, the ego, think how much time that this would take without the uplifting influence of greater knowledge to work himself out of it. Let us say someone became quite angry over something and proceeded to get sick. If this was something that was highly emotionally charged and would be added to something that was already buried in the sphere, then it could really have a long lasting impact in time. Now, think of this. If someone was sick for two weeks over this and could think of little else, then all of his energy would be devoted to extracting himself or working it out. Think how many weeks that you yourself would have gotten involved in your past life working out of certain depressive states. Can you remember a time when you may have been involved in one of these states for maybe up to three months?

*"Yes, I can remember those times."*

Now, you are in this lifetime. Think how many other lifetimes you may have spent working out details of other experiences. You could see, then, that the only escape would be to somehow work out the details of the lower self by its understanding so that you could gradually progress to the higher, more timeless aspect of thought. There is truth, then, to the statement, "You have all the time that you need." Do you understand this?

*"Yes, I understand. I may not like it, but I understand it."*

In other words, one will enter incarnations in time until the lessons set up by the soul are learned and then the soul would allow progression into higher ranges of thought until it again becomes as one, learning its part of the great schedule.

*"I have a question."*

Go ahead.

*"I and many others like me have always tended to be driven more from the right side of the brain than the left side. This has been very painful because it's impossible to explain that things do or don't feel right to people who are operating from the left side of the brain, because there has never been a logical explanation to give. My question is, is this planet set up, at this time, to be operating better for people who are accustomed to using the left side of the brain more than for us who are operating from the right? In other words, is this why I have always felt like a square peg trying to fit into a round hole?"*

You have brought up something of interest to many who would point out a need for this book in explaining why many would fit into the logical system set up some time ago, separating logic from intuition as a jumping off place for science. Remember when we were discussing intelligence tests?

*"Yes."*

We discussed that they measured certain functions that registered in the sphere but did not take into account someone who could at times bring in a greater part of their being and would bring forth greater intelligence if needed for some creative endeavor. If one could take such a test in one now moment and then take it in another now moment with another focus, the results would then change. There are many who could switch consciousness bringing their greater being into their consciousness which would influence such a result.

Take someone who was autistic, for instance. If they would be conditioned to painting, for example, they might paint with brilliance, but in attempting to connect to mundane activities, would be hopeless failures. The influence of education would be to help the average being to attain greater knowledge which would attempt to intersect the needs of many. There are those, however, who would already live from the more timeless side of themselves, who would therefore have some difficulty in adjusting to such a world. As consciousness would rise and the speed of thought would increase, then the need for different training would become much in evidence. How would you like to attend an intuition school?

*"I would love it."*

You have mentioned something, then, that would be of interest along the lines of limitation in the control of thought. Would you care to explain this?

*"I've heard so many times, 'We limit ourselves by our thinking,' but never fully understood it until the other day when we were talking to some people about their attempts to market their product. They were going to limit the use of it to a certain, selected few people."*

Yes, someone might invent something that would be of particular value to beings, but for some reason would decide to limit its use. If one would restrict the use, then of this machine in an artificial manner, seeking to keep its value to one's self, the universe seems to work in a fashion that would not allow this. What would happen, then, at a coincident time, another like kind of machine would be produced by someone else, maybe more than once, ensuring its distribution to those in need of it. This has happened over and over throughout your history with but little publicity. Sometimes an invention is created and will sit there for some time waiting for demand to catch up with its use. Some of your creations would fit into this category.

As you can see, then, in your future, I would already have another subject for a book, and that would be on timelessness.

One would be using thought as a constructive adjunct to gaining, then, the inner reaches of the mind that would not be governed by time.

How would you go about solving a problem, any problem?

*"It would depend on the degree of the problem."*

How about a problem of smoking?

*"With the problem of quitting smoking, I do not but ask for help. Quitting is so far beyond me that there is nothing else I*

*can do."*

How about a problem with money?

*"It's the same procedure with money. I just wait for it to come in. I've learned this the hard way. Planning and scheming to produce great amounts of money just didn't work, so I finally relaxed and that seems to work.*

*"It's usually necessary to take some action to solve problems, but the action usually turns out to be the opposite of what I would think would be effective. So, after many attempts to solve things by figuring out and effecting certain solutions that I think of and being disappointed in the results, I finally give up and then the problem gets solved in a way I never would have thought of."*

In essence, then, what I was trying to elicit from you would be to find out if you knew how to solve a problem. What this meant was, do you know how to raise your consciousness to let the timeless, smarter part of you solve the problem? Now, I have given you many different ways to attempt this, but let me explain another way.

If a problem comes up and you do not see the solution, then you can look for the solution by, first of all, seeing if you can let go of the solution. If you need a new car and the solution is not apparent, you would only go about pursuing the solution until the compulsive self, that is the false self, would jump in to render a fear solution. That is, it would imagine pieces flying out of your existing car and you being abandoned on the edge of a cliff with no escape. The false self would bring in fear and would then start finding problems with your existing car, pushing you even faster to solve the problem of getting a new one. You would know, with this example and any other, the compulsive, addictive self would have gained a foothold and then would instruct you falsely on how to accomplish what it fails to see, a solution. When you have gotten on to the emotional train, then you must stop it and get off or the solution can never manifest. Do you understand this?

*"I think so."*

This is very tricky. At the exact now moment that one would feel one's self slipping, pushing, forcing and otherwise trying to become the universe, then one would find one's self in the clutches of the ego.

The outside world then need be viewed as a friendly place that renders nothing but solutions. If you will try viewing it as your creation, which it is, it would but be the physical manifestation of thought.

If there would be prolonged period of dark weather which would seem to influence you, try shifting your focus to see if there is some purpose to it that would be greater than your own, for there always is. If you would have a friend or a neighbor who would be disturbing or irritating to you, try to view him as something of a solution looking for you to learn. If your children, for instance, would cause you undue stress, then there is some part of you that would need to learn what it is that is being pointed out. That is, there is some need within you that must be fulfilled. If one then would indulge in emotional reaction to such experience, it would then serve to postpone the time in the now moment that the completion of the experience would come about.

Now, one of the problems frequently encountered by beings is one of the clock, isn't it?

*"It has been a big problem for me."*

Where would you start if you chose to look at this?

*"I would try to figure out why I am habitually late."*

Now, maybe you would be in some other part of yourself when you would think of time, would you think?

*"Yes, I think of being on time as an activity of the left side of the brain and I operate from the right side."*

Now, don't get carried away. Where would you be, then, when you would be getting ready to be someplace?

*"Well, I wouldn't be in the now moment, that's for sure. I would be in a pattern that I set up a long time ago, a pattern of thinking that makes me late."*

How would this start out?

*"I would think that it would take less time to get ready and to travel to wherever I was going."*

Why would this be?

*"I would guess that it would be a sort of resentment at having to be at a certain place at a certain time."*

Do you know how to get out of this?

*"Obviously not."*

Change your pattern.

*"How would I do this?"*

Take a piece of paper and write down in a calm fashion, on the left side of the paper, how it is that you normally would prepare to be someplace that you agreed to be. Then, in the right column of the paper, write down how it really is. You would need to do this about three times after each experience of being late. What do you think this does?

*"Reveals to me why I'm making myself late."*

Now, I have tricked you, for what in essence you would be accomplishing is reprogramming your sphere in a way to ingroove new channels of thought using a different part of your sphere that would, in an unlimited way, allow you to view each experience as new or different which would result in viewing the problem from a higher focus. This would negate the old, lower, slower way of thinking and would provide you instant access to higher solutions on an ongoing basis.

Now, when you find a habitual pattern that would cause you difficulty, then it is a matter of reprogramming your use of a particular area of your sphere to have the solution rendered from a higher, more energetic, faster level. By use of this technique and by being openly willing to view it differently, then you can put the problem into solution by reprogramming the embedded chain of thought. You would then, in effect, rise above and let it solve itself. I cannot stress enough the importance leading up to this idea and would make every effort to encourage the reader to at least try it, for the results would be the reward.

What we would suggest, then, would be to control the lower, slower, emotion-clad thought and send it seeking a higher, brighter, faster, lighter solution which is a part of all beings.

# CHAPTER 11

## COMPOSITE

What are beings, then? Beings are collections of focused energy comprising thought which would catalog experience unique to each one, both in a timeless and timed framework. If one then would focus on that which would be known as a being out of time, one would view him as assembled particles of energy of various electrical charges which would result in the generation of frequencies, the collection of which would result in a unique vibration.

Now, the vibration of beings focused in a given time would be similar enough to allow them to communicate. Those of like kind would attract others of the same and these would be regarded as society or friends.

If a being would intersect in your time frame but would have the focus of another, difficulty in communication would then result. In order for me to communicate with you, I would then put forth a signal from timelessness intersecting your frequency and having the energy spelled out in linear time.

Since beings are in limited time and would focus in a linear fashion, then that which they are would result in confusion over the difference between past and future, but rarely resulting in the now moment. The resulting confusion between past and future, which is an illusion, would present difficulty in attempting to bring illusory energy or thought into the present moment. What beings are attempting is to bring that which isn't into the present and use it or that which will come into the present in the same manner. This results in distortion of time and would result in confusing degrees of communication which would be a factor of time. If someone would be speaking from 1922 and viewing it as today, then the confusing mixture of emotional charge would baffle the one with whom you would try to communicate.

Can you imagine the confusion if I were incarnated and came up to you with this conversation? "Hi, I am Seth. I live in 1922 and I will speak to you in 1998, your time. How are you today? Do you have a car?" Then the mythical being would answer, "Yes." And I would say, "Mine runs good with a top speed of thirty-five miles per hour." The mythical beings in 1998 would look at me like I was out of my mind, because his car would travel a good deal faster than that, and would view me as something strange, indeed. This sounds like something that could not happen. In actuality, this confusion takes place on a regular basis. Beings would tend to communicate on different illusory levels and would expect to be on the same frequency. The problem, then, would be the focus in time. Do you know what I mean?

*"We're not communicating what's really happening."*

This would at first appear to be confusing. But in essence, when beings communicate, for the most part, they would communicate, drawing their experience from a particular time which no longer exists. When the mother would communicate with the daughter and would attempt to have a meeting of the minds, this is difficult in that both would be viewing from a different aspect of time. The daughter would view her time couched in the energy closer to the present moment, but not in it, than the mother would, who is older and of a different time and energy. It is somewhat like having different incarnations speaking to each other. What I am saying here is that the energy of one will be of a different illusory nature, generally, than the illusory energy of another. Do you understand this?

*"It would be hard to miss, since, as you were speaking, my teenage daughter, Mia, walked in and we had a conversation which made no sense at all to either of us."*

She would communicate from one level of timed experience and you would communicate from another. No one is right or wrong, but the timing is different. If one would then become aware of this difference in thought energy, then the understanding of the communication would become clear.

Now, you could seek to communicate through her eyes, so to speak, and she would seek to communicate through yours. But what would result there is more confusion because the timed meanings of the words used would still result in a separation of understanding. The only resolution for communication difficulties such as these would be to bring both into the now moment so that one would communicate without benefit of time, except that of the now moment. Some terminology would be the same and you would then seek a common ground of understanding in the now moment. Both would have to view the communication as something new and fresh without benefit of experience to result in mutual understanding.

Do you know how you do this?

*"I would say to stay in the now moment, but I think there is something more to it."*

One would disconnect the emotional charge that one would have in communication, plus, as you said, stay in the now moment. But they would be one and the same, wouldn't they?

In dealing with beings in your society, it would be of great benefit to you to use intuition or feel in arriving at your area of thought in which to communicate with them. If you could view them as they are, as myriad color of thought and accurately bring this into your conscious focus, then communication problems would be greatly improved. For what would actually happen is that beings unknowingly would use this transmission of feeling and project their nuance of thought without benefit of spoken word.

Now, on this now moment, this would be a larger problem for beings to live or use, as you see it, than would first appear. Beings could listen to a channel and understand the feeling and for that period of time that they are connected, they would, in fact, be in the now moment, as you would experience. But as you so adroitly indicated, a few hours afterward, the same beings would escape the now moment and would reside elsewhere. Residing elsewhere, other than in the now moment, can then lead to many difficulties. This would be, then, a problem in or with time. One would be, in effect, in the wrong time.

Now, you have this friend who would tell you stories of the now moment. One that I overheard would be the one involving this young man and woman. When the couple first met, they fell in love and the feelings of bliss were so preponderant that all other emotion melted into insignificance. All thought, then, was selfless and the energy consumed them in a state of bliss. All was peace and happiness with the thought of each other. The birds sang, colors shone brightly and all things seemed wonderful. A sense of greatness filled the air and everything could be accomplished with little effort. The beings generally were in the now moment, for there was none other. After some time, the state of bliss subsided somewhat and the magnificent feeling that colored their vision became refocused in a way that their viewing of each other became one of a more critical nature. Upon looking at the other, a strange thing occurred. The former state of perfection that was viewed now became one of noticing faults in the other. It was viewed by this couple that over time, their feeling of closeness should change into a more regular relationship whereupon one's eyes were opened to the shortcomings of the other. In their past experience, both of themselves and from others, it would be viewed that this was the way. This way, then, would be cast in stone and forever unchangeable and would continue, no matter who they were involved with. What does this say to you?

*"Well, I think this is written for me, just as everyone else will think it is written for them."*

Why would you say that?

*"Because this is what happens to all of us. It is a rude shock and we always wish we could regain the magic we had in the beginning."*

This is a most interesting concept, for beings would have a time problem. Something happened to you recently that would be along this line, wouldn't it?

*"Yes, what a coincidence that is!"*

You would believe, then, that you would be focused a few years ahead and that your children would be grown up and you would be reduced to operating in a life filled with loneliness. You would perceive yourself living in this probable future, when you have no idea what the probable future would be. How would you feel and how would you think in the probable future, say six years hence?

*"I have no idea."*

Beings have but little insight into the probable future. Beings, then, would attempt to live in the probable future, based on their past experience, thereby doubling the illusion. As I have said, all that beings have is the now moment. The rest is illusion and would have the effect of robbing you of your energy!

If one then would view each now moment as unique unto itself and that now moment would never be repeated, then one would disconnect past experience from future events. What I am leading up to is stating that all is created by you now. This is what I meant by saying that beings would have a time problem in living in the past or the future instead of now.

Now, let us take your example, for instance. When you would take your previous experience, which is thought, and project it into the future, you would take negative energy and increase the emotional charge and have it play the record as you would suppose it to be in the probable future. What would happen, then, with such a distorted view of reality, would be to render you into a state of depression of a heavy energy that would incapacitate you. By your own thought, then, you would create an illusion that would drain your energy. This might seem to be something that would rarely happen to beings, but in essence, this takes place a high percentage of time in the lives of most beings. How could one take, then, the past and project it into the future, living there falsely and then perceive it as reality? On the surface, it would seem to be impossible. But if you would believe that your thought is reality, then life is as you create it.

Let us take the couple, then, who would take their experience and attempt to blend it into their reality. If the couple would choose to continue to treat each now moment as unique unto itself, allowing no interference from experience, then their feelings of happiness need never dissipate. This is a difficult concept to explain. In the now moment, there is no dissipation of energy. Feelings then do not change in the now moment. Affection is of the now moment. If a couple, then, would be once happy, then they can always be happy in the now moment. What happens, however, is that one or the other would decide to begin thinking of more important events, such as their financial condition or the condition of some material object and would begin to worry, bringing into focus past experience and future fear.

When we were discussing a change brought about by a ringing telephone, you would see, then, my attempt to teach beings to stay in the present moment and not be influenced by triggers which would bring in the past and the future. It would seem by now that I would get carried away in this discussion and would be deemed repetitious and mundane. But you brought up a point, didn't you? And that would be the reason for repetition. And what would that be?

*"These points have to be repeated and repeated, because we cannot hear them."*

Someone might make a disparaging remark to you, something about your appearance, for instance. How long do you think this would stay on your mind?

*"It would depend on what was said."*

How about wrinkles?

*"I don't have any!"*

Yes, I know, but what if they said this?

*"I would do some close examination, maybe stand on my head an hour a day to increase blood circulation, maybe buy some new cosmetics. At the least, I would probably worry."*

Beings are going to make negative comments to you every so often. It would seem a better way for you not to take them in. You might, then, without emotion, think that perhaps their eyes have not been examined for some time and perhaps they would need some new glasses. Maybe something is wrong with their seeing. You needn't get carried away and think, "I am a great beauty and how could they not see this?" Kidding, of course. The truth being that one's focus would be from different levels at different times and if they would see you one way one day and another way another day, you might suspect that they might color their thoughts from certain focuses, resulting in distortion, one way or the other.

An exercise that would be of interest to those who would care to remain in the now moment, would be one of setting an alarm for ten minutes, merely ten minutes of your time. Within that ten minute span, have some paper and a pencil in your hand and each time that you would wander into the past or future, put a mark on the paper and at the end of ten minutes, count the marks.

*"It's going to be solid marks."*

Unless you made a concerted effort to meditate or otherwise stay in the now moment, you would indeed find many marks on the paper. A variation of this would be to have two columns on the paper, one past and one future and see what the net result would be. Try to monitor your conversation, as you suggested, and speak of nothing but what is now, nothing out of the past, nothing out of the future and see how difficult this is.

*"It would be a short conversation."*

When you laugh, are you in the past or the future?

*"You're in the now moment."*

Yes. When you touch someone, transferring your energy, then this would put you and them in the now moment.

There are many who can take a fearful or suspenseful situation and remove the emotional charge by making a joke. Humor then will bring all into the now moment, releasing the charged experience. So now we have added other elements to our sphere. That would be the past, present or future influence upon the charged thought. The now moment would be the worm hole or escape into the present, bypassing the emotional charge into the unlimited area of thought. The solution, then, is in the present. Does that make sense to you?

*"Sorry, would you repeat that question? I was thinking of something else."*

I thought so.

So now tying in the components of this book, such as variables and blocks and colors and/or hues, to the influence of the now moment would be our mission. First we have learned how to pull out past influence and future fear by a variety of methods. Then we learned that by staying in the now moment, we can bypass them. This is not to say that weeding the garden, so to speak, would not have benefit. If one is so encased in emotional drama that one is incapable of pulling oneself out of it, it would behoove him to weave his way out of his negative experience. It is only then, when one has weeded the garden, so to speak, from the heavy thought energy, can one then begin to experience the now moment on a consistent basis. Initially, one would begin to experience or feel the now moment a small percentage of available time. Then, as one progresses, the percentage is increased gradually until one would tie oneself into the now moment on a consistent basis, guarding against flipping backward into time. This would take consistent practice to avoid attaching to results and past experience.

Many would try tricks, as you would suggest, tying a string around their wrist or finger to remind them to stay centered, or in the now moment. John tried something imaginative at one time, where he took a ball of string and each time a negative thought was pulled out of his sphere or experience, then he would unravel it a few inches. Guess what happened?

*"He ran out of string."*

Yes. Almost all would run out of string, for with some fifteen thousand thoughts per day, some of which would be negative, one would need a ball of string perhaps one hundred feet high.

*"And that's on a good day!"*

Joking, of course. The way would be to pull out many of the heavier, charged, negative variety and then proceed to enlist the aid of the now moment. There would be others, then, who would hang a now sign in every room of the house, but pretty soon, it would be as the wall itself and no one would see it. The easiest way, then, would be to practice bringing yourself back into the now, such as with true tunnel vision, or focusing on the here and now.

# CHAPTER 12

## THE END RESULT

Beings in this time are facing a changing world, a world that would be as those in other civilizations. With increased technology, we have already seen a machine that will measure part of the subconscious or that which is not available to you as separated beings. This would be just the beginning. There are those who are now being incarnated who would have advanced ability to read others' thoughts. This would not have the negative connotation that might first appear. Already, most beings would accomplish this, but without their knowing. Most communication, then, would be nonverbal and the spoken word, as we have discovered, would have little meaning except as a telephone line or a vehicle used to carry energy, which then becomes synergy.

There are already cases where the information would suggest that beings are communicating telepathically without spoken language. As greater energy would come in with the growth of this planet, then technology would increase, necessitating better ways of communicating. If technology then would increase, then language as symbols would be a limiting factor. The use of a communication stemming from the timeless part of the sphere would be useful in speeding up transmission of images or energy in a way that knowing, instead of what you would regard as thinking, would become of use. When something of knowing is transmitted, then words would not suffice. Beings will learn to reroute their thinking as you now know it, to a lighter, brighter variety.

The word "thinking" then would be limited and would be used as a limited function in a logical sense. Number storage would come to mind or name storage or storage of useful ideas which would be labeled as I have labeled thought.

In effect, in the probable future, one would begin thinking one's way into knowing or knowingness. You could say that thought would be speeded up into knowing. Knowing then would be at infinite speed and would supercede thought. Knowing then would be translated into thought which would be of time. The old adage, time is of the essence, would then apply as limitation. You see, you really do not think anything out, in effect. The end result, then, is that you think your way into knowing or infinity, which then solves the problem, translating it back into thought in time, which would imply limitation or linearity.

What beings then would learn, hopefully from this book, is to translate their thought into higher knowing or images which would project at infinite speed. Infinite speed then could not be translated into words and therefore, a different form of communication would result. The need for names then would eventually be limited. It would only be then that limited thought would be used as a last resort to communicate what could not be communicated in the real sense. Thought then would take on the aspects of illusion and would be this in fact. Naturally, beings at this stage of evolution would be somewhat different than now. Probably, I have taken this far enough in the probable future because the limitations of thought would stop us there. Can you imagine living in a non-verbal world?

"No."

Does it seem like much fun?

"No."

Each then would have his chosen time of expression and the time of the probable future is beyond your imagination and would not seem an enjoyable place. Beings in this time frame would clearly be out of place and time and would have little interest in living in an environment where even communication is different. You can thus see how beings are limited by their thinking. This would be an age, then, where beings are beginning to know and would need an acceleration of consciousness to be in the know. It is all energy, however, and since energy takes many different forms, it would only be a function of time. It will be some of your probable time before the advent of the age of knowing and even this will not be the end of it, probably.

Prior to the age of knowing, one would need to use thought to propel oneself above heavier thought. One would gradually progress up the scale to higher and higher energy where lighter, brighter thought would reside. One would live from a higher level and then would use thought in a stairstep fashion to propel oneself higher and higher until the non-verbal, non-thinking stage would be reached.

The advent of direct telephathic communication would necessitate the cleaning of interconnecting thought at lower levels. That is, one must let go of this lower energy to enable oneself to communicate at sufficient speed for telepathy to be effective. It is a self-correcting mechanism in that the lower energy will not project as well as the higher thought energy. One could not use telepathy to project anger, for instance, over any distance, for the factor of time would slow it down. One could not be destructive with knowing, for then the knowing could not be transmitted. It would just weigh too much. Would you like to weigh your anger by the pound? Can you imagine this mythical conversation? "Hi, Sam. How are you today? Would you like my five pounds of fear?" And Sam would say, "No, thank you. But would you take my six pounds of anger?" If one then has cleared up his lower energy thought, then one could feel free to have others intersect with one's mind to read it. No one then would worry about this, for all that would be read would be of a lighter, brighter nature. So one would not be in a civilization of mind readers until the mind were cleaned up enough so that it could be read. It would not be that one couldn't read the black thoughts, but who would want to? They would see something heavy and ominous and dark lying there and would know that they didn't want any part of it and would seek to shield themselves from it.

When one would be in the now moment and would strike from the focus of knowing, then one could project light, bright access variables that would see around corners. What this means is that when one had access to a high enough level, then one would bring into focus that which one would know as precognition. You would see then where there is no time and space and would bring in information that was right there, even though it would be some distance in time and space.

Each level, then, of new knowledge is brought forth in time to allow beings to adjust to the higher energy. Beings would get overwhelmed if they received too much energy or knowledge too quickly. The conscious mind would be overwhelmed and being in time, it would need time to adjust. This is one of the reasons that generally beings would not have the remotest idea of what would take place in the future. If one were to project oneself to living in the future, it would only take one special invention that would change the course of time. Such inventions would be beyond the conscious mind to imagine.

Let us say that someone invented a machine that would in some way get you around the blocks of limitation and would give you access to greater intelligence and technology that would have you living as you would but twenty years from now. Would you be happy?

*"Probably not because you wouldn't match the rest of the world."*

How about masters?

*"They're happy."*

They would have advanced themselves to higher understanding and would be able to live from the level of knowing. This could be a dual question, couldn't it?

*"Yes."*

They could live from advanced understanding and be happy there and could be happy in this time because they're out of time. Since happiness comes from within, they probably would not even be lonely, would they? There would be so many reasons for letting go of false images known as emotion that if one were thinking of it, it would not even take a second thought. The problem, as we have seen, is that if one would have the tools to let go of lower energy thoughts, one would forget to use them. If a being would continue to practice being in the now moment and let go of past experience, then this would be the quickest way to grow. Many have stated that it is but a problem of remembering, not of forgetting. If one could remember who he is, then one would soon forget who he assumes he is. Once one gets into the knowing of the now moment, one would soon forget the illusionary ex-